GHOST
HUNTER

TARCHER SUPERNATURAL LIBRARY

Isis in America by Henry Steel Olcott

The Romance of Sorcery by Sax Rohmer

Ghost Hunter by Hans Holzer

TARCHER
SUPER-
NATURAL
LIBRARY

JEREMY P. TARCHER/PENGUIN
a member of Penguin Group (USA)
New York

GHOST
HUNTER

The Groundbreaking Classic

—— of ——

Paranormal Investigation

♆

HANS HOLZER

3 1571 00325 7725

JEREMY P. TARCHER/PENGUIN
Published by the Penguin Group
Penguin Group (USA) LLC
375 Hudson Street
New York, New York 10014

USA · Canada · UK · Ireland · Australia
New Zealand · India · South Africa · China

penguin.com
A Penguin Random House Company

Ghost Hunter was originally published in 1963.
First Jeremy P. Tarcher/Penguin edition 2014

Most Tarcher/Penguin books are available at special quantity discounts for bulk
purchase for sales promotions, premiums, fund-raising, and educational needs.
Special books or book excerpts also can be created to fit specific needs.
For details, write: Special.Markets@us.penguingroup.com.

Library of Congress Cataloging-in-Publication Data

Holzer, Hans, 1920–2009.
Ghost hunter: the groundbreaking classic of paranormal investigation / Hans Holzer.
p.   cm.—(Tarcher supernatural library; 1)
ISBN 978-0-399-16921-2
1. Ghosts—New York (State)—New York.   2. Parapsychology.
3. Holzer, Hans, 1920–2009.   I. Title.
BF1472.U6H63733   2014   2014012316
133.109747—dc23

Printed in the United States of America
1 3 5 7 9 10 8 6 4 2

Book design by Meighan Cavanaugh

CONTENTS

GHOST HUNTER

INTRODUCTION: GHOSTS, ANYONE?

As a professional ghost hunter, I am forever on the lookout for likely prospects. There is no dearth of haunted houses in Manhattan. There is, however, a king-sized amount of shyness among witnesses to ghostly phenomena which keeps me from getting what I am after. Occasionally, this shyness prevents me from investigating a promising case.

There was a man, on Long Island, who was appalled at the idea of my bringing a medium to his house. Even though he did not question my integrity as a psychic investigator, he decided to discuss the matter with his bishop. Mediums and such are the work of the Devil, the cleric sternly advised the owner of the haunted house, and permission for my visit was withdrawn.

Although the "poltergeist" case of Seaford, Long Island,

had been in all the papers, and even on national television, the idea of a volunteer medium trying to help solve the mystery proved too much for the prejudiced owner of the house.

Then, there was the minister who carefully assured me that there couldn't be anything to the rumors I'd heard about footsteps and noises when there wasn't anyone there. What he meant, of course, was that he *preferred* it that way. Still, that was one more potential case I lost before even getting to first base. Don't get me wrong—these people understand who I am; they have respect for my scientific credentials; and they know their anonymity will be carefully guarded. They know I'm not a crackpot or an amateur—amusing himself with something he does not understand. In fact, they're very much interested to hear all about these things, provided it happened in *someone else's* house.

I am a professional investigator of ghosts, haunted houses, and other "spontaneous" phenomena, to use the scientific term—that is, anything of a supernormal nature, not fully explained by orthodox happenings, and thus falling into the realm of parapsychology or psychic research.

I wasn't born a ghost hunter. I grew up to be one, from very early beginnings, though. At the age of three, in my native Vienna, my *Kindergarten* teacher threatened me with expulsion from the class for telling ghost stories to my wide-eyed classmates. These, however, were the non-evidential kind of stories I had made out of whole cloth. Still, it showed I was hot on the subject, even then!

Even in Freudian Vienna, ghost-story telling is not considered a gainful profession, so my schooling prepared me for the more orthodox profession of being a writer. I managed to major in history and archeology, knowledge I found extremely helpful in my later research work, for it taught me the methods of painstaking corroboration and gave me a kind of bloodhound approach in the search for facts. The fact that I was born under the truth-seeking sign of Aquarius made all this into a way of life for me.

I am the Austrian-born son of a "returnee" from New York; thus I grew up with an early expectation of returning to New York as soon as I was old enough to do so. Meanwhile, I lived like any other child of good family background, alternately sheltered and encouraged to express myself.

I had barely escaped from *Kindergarten* when my thoughtful parents enrolled me in a public school one year ahead of my time. It took hundreds of dollars and a special *ukase* by the Minister of Education to get me in at that early age of five, but it was well worth it to my suffering parents.

I had hardly warmed the benches of my first-grade class when I started to build radio sets, which in those days were crystal powered. For the moment, at least, ghosts were not in evidence. But the gentle security into which I had lulled my elders was of brief duration. I had hardly turned nine when I started to write poems, dramas (all of four pages)— and, you're right—ghost stories. Only now they had more terror in them, since I had absorbed a certain amount of mayhem, thanks to the educational motion pictures we were treated to in those days and certain literary sources known as Zane Grey and Karl May.

My quaint writings earned me the reputation of being "special," without giving me any compensation of fame or fortune.

Gradually, girls began to enter my world. This fact did not shatter my imaginative faculties. It simply helped populate my ghost stories with more alluring female ghosts.

I was now about thirteen or fourteen, and frequently visited my late Uncle Henry in his native city of Bruenn. My Uncle Henry was as "special" as was I, except that his career as a businessman had restricted his unusual interests to occasional long talks and experiments. In his antique-filled room in my grandparents' house, we held weird rites which we called the "raising of the spirits," and which, for all we knew, might have raised a spirit or two. We never waited around long enough to find out, but turned the lights back on when it got too murky. Needless to say, we also indulged in candle rites and readings from my uncle's substantial collection of occult books.

I didn't think my uncle ever believed in the occult, but many years later, just before his passing, he did confess to me that he had no doubts about the reality of "the other world" and spirit communication. If I am to believe several professional and nonprofessional mediums who have since brought me messages from him, he is now in a position of proving this reality to himself, and to me.

In 1935 I was fifteen and I had become a collector of

antiques and coins and was an ardent bibliophile. One day, while digging through the stacks at a bookseller's, I came across an early, but then rather up-to-date account of the scientific approach to the occult, called *Occultism in This Modern Age*. It was the work of Dr. T. K. Oesterreich, a professor at the University of Tübingen in Germany. This 1928 book started me off on a serious approach to ghosts.

At first, it was idle curiosity mixed with a show-me kind of skepticism. I read other books, journals, and learned bulletins. But I didn't attend any seances or have any actual contact with the subject while a teen-ager. My training at this point veered toward the newspaper-writing profession.

I took a course in practical journalism, and started to sell articles to local papers. The reportorial training added the "interview in depth" approach to my later investigations. All this time, we had dreamed of coming back to New York, of which my father had fond memories. But it wasn't until 1938, when I had just turned eighteen, that I set foot on American soil. My first job had nothing to do with occultism, and it paid only fifteen dollars weekly in a day when that was just enough to live on uncomfortably.

Falling back (or forward, if you wish) on my knowledge of antiquities and coins, I became an expert cataloguer and writer for one of the big importers of such things.

In 1945 I quit my position—I was then associate editor of a scientific magazine dealing with coins and antiquities—and I became a free-lance writer. My old interest in the occult revived; the flame had never died but had been dormant, and now it burst forth again. More books, more lectures, more seeking out the unorthodox, the tantalizingly unsolved.

In 1949 I went to Europe as an accredited foreign correspondent, with the intent to write articles on cultural activities, the theater, and human-interest stories. I had begun to write plays and compose music myself, a skill which I have since used professionally in the New York theater. On this trip, which led me from the heel of the boot of Italy to the northern part of Sweden, I realized that much psychic research activity was going on in the countries I visited. However, the brevity of my stay in each place precluded any close contact with these bodies.

The following year I returned to Europe, again as a foreign correspondent. In this capacity, I covered the theater in London and other major cities of Europe. One evening, I was invited backstage at the Hippodrome Theatre in London, where comedian Michael Bentine was then appearing as one of the stars. Mr. Bentine offered me a home-grown tomato instead of a drink: he immediately ingratiated himself to me since I am a vegetarian. It also developed that Michael and I had birthdays on the same day, though a few years apart. A friendship grew quickly between us, especially when we discovered our common interest in the occult.

I remember we had a luncheon date in one of London's Spanish restaurants. Luncheon was served at twelve noon, conversation started at one, and at five o'clock the owner gently tiptoed over to us and whispered, "Dinner is being prepared!"

When I returned home that night, I started to work on a television series based on actual hauntings. Through mutual friends, I was led to a study group composed of earnest young people from various walks of life, who meet regularly in the rooms belonging to the Edgar Cayce Foundation in New York. Their purpose was simply the quest for truth in the vast realm of extrasensory perception. From then on, I devoted more and more time and energies to this field.

One of the greatest of all living mediums and, at the same time, psychic researchers is Eileen Garrett, who is today president of the Parapsychology Foundation of New York, a world-wide organization that encourages and supports truly scientific investigations and studies in the realm of extrasensory perception. The Foundation also publishes magazines, and has helped the publication of important books on psychic subjects.

I had met Mrs. Garrett briefly in 1946 without realizing that she was the same person whose psychic reputation had long awed me. The contact with her became stronger after my return from Europe in 1951, when I discussed my work and ideas on psychic research with her from time to time.

Eileen Garrett had no patience with guesswork or make-believe. She taught me to be cautious and painstaking, so that the results of my research would not be open to question. My friendship with Eileen Garrett helped a great deal. Since she was both a great medium and researcher, I adopted her severe approach. I neither believed nor disbelieved; I looked only for facts, no matter what the implications.

At the Edgar Cayce Foundation on 16th Street and elsewhere, I also met the handful of nonprofessional mediums who helped me so much in my investigations. My method frequently calls for the presence of a sensitive person to pick up clairvoyantly, or through trance, tangible material about a haunted house, that could then later be examined for veracity. I don't hold with the ghost hunter who spends a night alone in a haunted house, and then has nothing more to show for his bravery than a stiff back.

To me, the purpose of investigation is twofold; one, to establish the observed facts of the phenomena, and two, to make contact with the alleged ghost. The chances of seeing an apparition, if you're not sensitive yourself, are nil, and I don't like to waste time.

"Ghosts" are people, or part of people, anyway, and thus governed by emotional stimuli; they do not perform like trained circus animals, just to please a group of skeptics or sensation seekers. Then too, one should remember that an apparition is really a re-enactment of an earlier emotional experience, and rather a personal matter. A sympathetic visitor would encourage it; a hostile onlooker inhibit it.

Sometimes an "ordinary" person does manage to see or hear a ghost in an allegedly haunted location, be it a building or open space. Such a person is of course sensitive or mediumistic, without knowing it, and this is less unusual than one might think.

Even though I am an artistic, and therefore sensitive, person, I do not profess to mediumship, and certainly would not be satisfied with the meager impressions I might gather myself, psychically. A more advanced psychic talent is very necessary to get results. So, I take my "sensitive" with me. If I also see or hear some unearthly things, well and good. That's a bonus. But I don't like unfinished cases. And rarely indeed have I come home empty-handed when I set out in the company of a good medium.

Are good mediums hard to find? They are! That is why I spend a considerable portion of my efforts in this field in search for good new mediums. These are people with the extrasensory gift, whose interest is scientific, not financial. Natural talents in this field, just as in any other, can be trained. There are strict methods and conditions, and when you work in a field that is still on the fringes of recognized science, the more stringent your conditions are, the better.

Today, my methods are well thought out. When I hear of a likely case or prospect, I call the owners or tenants of the building, or if an open area, the nearest neighbor or potential witness, and introduce myself. I get as much information as I can on witnesses and type of phenomena observed, then call the witnesses and interview them. Only after this preliminary work has been done do I call in one of my sensitive-collaborators. I tell them only that a case has come up, and when I will need them.

I discuss everything *but the case* with them on our way to the location, and when we get there, the hosts have been informed not to volunteer any information, either.

A good medium like Mrs. Ethel Meyers will immediately get "impressions" upon arriving, and sometimes even on the way toward our goal. A little later, she will lapse into a trance, and in this condition, the alleged ghost can operate her vocal cords, and speak to me directly.

Sometimes there is another sitter present, and sometimes not. I take notes or use a tape recorder, or both. And sometimes, too, there is an infrared camera present, just in case.

After the trance is over, the medium awakens without remembering anything that has just come through her mouth or vocal cords while under the control of an alleged ghost. Sometimes, though not often, the medium recalls all or part of the information thus received because the trance had been light. This does not mean the medium is faking, or that the material obtained is less reliable; it only means that the medium's trance faculties are not in full operating condition, and perhaps hypnosis is in order to get her "down deeper" into the unconscious condition. Generally speaking, the medium remembers nothing of what went on during her trance state.

Now I allow the hosts and other sitters to discuss the case freely and comment upon what they have just heard or witnessed. Often enough, corroboration takes place right then and there, but more often I have to dig it up in the public library, special libraries, or other sources to which I have access. The research always takes place after the investigation is closed. The Sensitive is never kept abreast of the progress of the corroboration until the case is ready for publication or filing.

There is always drama, and sometimes comedy, involved. Ghosts are people, haunted by unhappy memories, and incapable of escaping by themselves from the vicious net of emotional entanglements. It's not a good idea for a ghost hunter to be afraid of *anything,* because fear attracts undesirables even among the Unseen.

An authoritative and positive position is quite essential with both medium and ghost. Sometimes, these "entities" or visitors in temporary control of the medium's speech mechanism like their newly found voice so much, they don't want to leave. That's when the firm orders of the Investigator alone send them out of the medium's body.

There are dangers involved in this work, but only for the *amateur.* For a good psychic researcher does know how to rid the medium of unwanted entities. If all this sounds like a medieval text to you, hold your judgment. You may not have seen a "visitor" take over a Sensitive's body, and "operate" it the way you might operate a car! But I have, and other researchers have, and when the memories are those of the alleged ghost, and certainly not those of the medium, then you can't dismiss such things as fantastic!

Too much disbelieving is just as unscientific as too much believing. Even though the lady in T. S. Eliot's *Confidential Clerk* says blandly, "I don't believe in facts," I do. Facts—come to think of it—are the only things I really *do* believe in.

THE
BANK STREET
GHOST

On June 26, 1957, I picked up a copy of *The New York Times,* that most unghostly of all newspapers, and soon was reading Meyer Berger's column, "About New York." That column wasn't about houses or people this particular day. It was about ghosts.

Specifically, Mr. Berger gave a vivid description of a house at 11 Bank Street, in Greenwich Village, where a "rather friendly" ghost had apparently settled to share the appointments with the flesh-and-blood occupants. The latter were Dr. Harvey Slatin, an engineer, and his wife, Yeffe Kimball, who is of Osage Indian descent and well known as a painter.

The house in which they lived was then 125 years old, made of red brick, and still in excellent condition.

Digging into the past of their home, the Slatins

established that a Mrs. Maccario had run the house as a nineteen-room boarding establishment for years before selling it to them. However, Mrs. Maccario wasn't of much help when questioned. She knew nothing of her predecessors.

After the Slatins had acquired the house, and the other tenants had finally left, they did the house over. The downstairs became one long living room, extending from front to back, and adorned by a fireplace and a number of good paintings and ceramics. In the back part of this room, the Slatins placed a heavy wooden table. The rear door led to a small garden, and a narrow staircase led to the second floor.

The Slatins were essentially "uptown" people, far removed from any Bohemian notions or connotations. What attracted them about Greenwich Village was essentially its quiet charm and artistic environment. They gathered around them friends of similar inclinations, and many an evening was—and is—spent "just sitting around," enjoying the tranquil mood of the house.

During these quiet moments, they often thought they heard a woman's footsteps on the staircase, sometimes crossing the upper floors, sometimes a sound like a light hammering. Strangely enough, the sounds were heard more often in the daytime than at night, a habit most unbecoming a traditional haunt. The Slatins were never frightened by this. They simply went to investigate what might have caused the noises, but never found any visible evidence. There was no "rational" explanation for them, either. One Sunday in January of 1957, they decided to clock the noises, and found that the ghostly goings-on lasted all day; during these hours, they would run upstairs to trap the trespasser—only to find empty rooms and corridors. Calling out to the Unseen brought no reply, either. An English carpenter by the name of Arthur Brodie was as well adjusted to reality as are the Slatins, but he also heard the footsteps. His explanation that "one hears all sorts of noises in old houses" did not help matters any. Sadie, the maid, heard the noises too, and after an initial period of panic, got accustomed to them as if they were part of the house's routine—which indeed they were!

One morning in February, Arthur Brodie was working in a room on the top floor, hammering away at the ceiling. He was standing on a stepladder that allowed him to just about touch the ceiling. Suddenly, plaster and dust showered down on his head, and something heavy fell and hit the floor below. Mrs. Slatin in her first-floor bedroom heard the thump. Before she could investigate the source of the loud noise, there was Brodie at her door, saying: "It's me, Ma'am, Brodie. I'm leaving the job! I've found the body!" But he was being facetious. What he actually found was a black-painted metal container about twice the size of a coffee can. On it there was a partially faded label, reading: *"The last remains of Elizabeth Bullock, deceased. Cremated January 21, 1931."* The label also bore the imprint of the United States Crematory Company, Ltd., Middle Village, Borough of Queens, New York, and stamped on the top of the can was the number—37251. This can is in the Slatins' house to this very day.

Mrs. Slatin, whose Indian forebears made her accept the supernatural without undue alarm or even amazement, quietly took the find, and called her husband at his office. Together with Brodie, Dr. Slatin searched the hole in the ceiling, but found only dusty rafters.

Curiously, the ceiling that had hidden the container dated back at least to 1880, which was long before Elizabeth Bullock had died. One day, the frail woman crossed Hudson Street, a few blocks from the Slatin residence. A motorist going at full speed saw her too late, and she was run over. Helpful hands carried her to a nearby drugstore, while other by-standers called for an ambulance. But help arrived too late for Mrs. Bullock. She died at the drugstore before any medical help arrived. But strangely enough, when Dr. Slatin looked through the records, he found that Mrs. Bullock had never lived at 11 Bank Street at all!

Still, Mrs. Bullock's ashes were found in that house. How to explain that? In the crematory's books, her home address was listed at 113 Perry Street. Dr. Slatin called on Charles Dominick, the undertaker in the case. His place of business had been on West 11th Street, not far from Bank Street. Unfortunately, Mr. Dominick had since died.

The Slatins then tried to locate the woman's relatives, if any. The trail led nowhere. It was as if the ghost of the deceased wanted to protect her secret. When the search seemed hopeless, the Slatins put the container with Mrs. Bullock's ashes on the piano in the large living room, feeling somehow that Mrs. Bullock's ghost might prefer that place of honor to being cooped up in the attic. They got so used to it that even Sadie, the maid, saw nothing extraordinary in dusting it right along with the rest of the furniture and bric-a-brac.

Still, the Slatins hoped that someone would claim the ashes sooner or later. Meanwhile, they considered themselves the custodians of Mrs. Bullock's last remains. And apparently they had done right by Elizabeth, for the footsteps and disturbing noises stopped abruptly when the can was found and placed on the piano in the living room.

One more strange touch was told by Yeffe Kimball to the late Meyer Berger. It seems that several weeks before the ashes of Mrs. Bullock were discovered, someone rang the doorbell and inquired about rooms. Mrs. Slatin recalls that it was a well-dressed young man, and that she told him they would not be ready for some time, but that she would take his name in order to notify him when they were. The young man left a card, and Mrs. Slatin still recalls vividly the name on it. It was E. C. Bullock. Incidentally, the young man never did return.

It seems odd that Mrs. Slatin was not more nonplussed by the strange coincidence of the Bullock name on the container and card, but, as I have already stated, Mrs. Slatin is quite familiar with the incursions from the Nether World that are far more common than most of us would like to think. To her, it seemed something odd, yes, but also something that no doubt would "work itself out." She was neither disturbed nor elated over the continued presence in her living room of Mrs. Bullock's ashes. Mrs. Slatin is gifted with psychic talents, and therefore not afraid of the

Invisible. She takes the Unseen visitors as casually as the flesh-and-blood ones, and that is perhaps the natural way to look at it, after all.

Greenwich Village has so many haunted or allegedly haunted houses that a case like the Slatins' does not necessarily attract too much attention from the local people. Until Meyer Berger's interview appeared in the *Times*, not many people outside of the Slatins' immediate circle of friends knew about the situation.

Mr. Berger, who was an expert on Manhattan folklore, knew the Slatins, and also knew about ghosts. He approached the subject sympathetically, and the Slatins were pleased. They had settled down to living comfortably in their ghost house, and since the noises had stopped, they gave the matter no further thought.

I came across the story in the *Times* in June of 1957, and immediately decided to follow up on it. I don't know whether my friend and medium, Mrs. Ethel Meyers, also read the article; it is possible that she did. At any rate, I told her nothing more than that a haunted house existed in the Village and she agreed to come with me to investigate it. I then called the Slatins and, after some delay, managed to arrange for a seance to take place on July 17th, 1957, at 9:30 P.M. Present were two friends of the Slatins, Mr. and Mrs. Anderson, Meyer Berger, the Slatins, Mrs. Meyers, and myself.

Immediately upon entering the house and sitting down at the table, around which we had grouped ourselves, Mrs. Meyers went into trance. Just as she "went under" and was still in that borderline condition where clairvoyance touches true trance, she described the presence of a little woman who walked slowly, being paralyzed on one side, and had a heart condition. "She's Betty," Mrs. Meyers murmured, as she "went under." Now the personality of "Betty" started to use the vocal apparatus of the medium.

Our medium continued in her trance state: "He didn't want me in the family plot—my brother—I wasn't even married in their eyes. . . . But I was married before God . . . Edward Bullock. . . . I want a Christian burial in the shades of the Cross—any place where the cross is—*but not with them!*" This was said with so much hatred and emotion that I tried to persuade the departed Betty to desist, or at least to explain her reasons for not wishing to join her family in the cemetery.

"I didn't marry in the faith," she said, and mentioned that her brother was Eddie, that they came from Pleasantville, New York, and that her mother's maiden name was Elizabeth McCuller. "I'm at rest now," she added in a quieter mood.

How did her ashes come to be found in the attic of a house that she never even lived in?

"I went with Eddie," Betty replied. "There was a family fight . . . my husband went with Eddie . . . steal the ashes . . . pay for no burial . . . he came back and took them from Eddie . . . hide ashes . . . Charles knew it . . . made a roof over the house . . . ashes came through the roof . . . so Eddie can't find them . . ."

I asked, were there any children?

"Eddie and Gracie. Gracie died as a baby, and Eddie now lives in California. Charlie protects me!" she added, referring to her husband.

At this point I asked the departed what was the point of staying on in this house now? Why not go on into the Great World Beyond, where she belonged? But evidently the ghost didn't feel that way at all! "I want a cross over my head . . . have two lives to live now . . . and I like being with you!" she said, bowing toward Mrs. Slatin. Mrs. Slatin smiled. She didn't mind in the least having a ghost as a boarder. "What about burial in your family plot?" That would seem the best, I suggested. The ghost became vehement.

"Ma never forgave me. I can never go with her and rest. I don't care much. When she's forgiven me, maybe it'll be all right . . . only where there's a green tree cross—and where there's no more fighting over the bones . . . I want only to be set free, and there should be peace. . . . I never had anything to do with them. . . . Just because I loved a man out of the faith, and so they took my bones and fought over them, and then they put them up in this place, and let them smoulder up there, so nobody could touch them . . . foolish me! When they're mixed up with the Papal State. . . ."

Did her husband hide the ashes all by himself?

"There was a Peabody, too. He helped him."

Who cremated her?

"It was Charles' wish, and it wasn't Eddie's and there-fore, they quarreled. Charlie was a Presbyterian . . . and he would have put me in his Church, but I could not offend them all. They put it beyond my reach through the roof; still hot . . . they stole it from the crematory."

Where was your home before, I asked.

"Lived close by," she answered, and as if to impress upon us again her identity, added—"Bullock!"

Throughout the seance, the ghost had spoken with a strong Irish brogue. The medium's background is not Irish, and I have a fine ear for authenticity of language, perhaps because I speak seven of them, and can recognize many more. This was not the kind of brogue a clever actor puts on. This was a real one.

As the entranced medium served the cause of Mrs. Bullock, I was reminded of the time I first heard the tape recordings of what became later known as Bridie Murphy. I remember the evening when the author of *The Search for Bridie Murphy,* Morey Bernstein, let me and a small group of fellow researchers in on an exciting case he had recently been working on. The voice on the tape, too, had an authentic Irish brogue, and a flavor no actor, no matter how brilliant, could fully imitate!

Now the medium seemed limp—as the ghost of Elizabeth Bullock withdrew. A moment later, Mrs. Meyers awoke, none the worse for having been the link between two worlds.

After the seance, I suggested to Mrs. Slatin that the can containing the ashes be buried in her garden, beneath the tree I saw through the back window. But Mrs. Slatin wasn't sure. She felt that her ghost was just as happy to stay on the piano.

I then turned my attention to Mrs. Slatin herself, since she admitted to being psychic. A gifted painter, Yeffe Kimball *knew* that Mrs. Meyers had made the right contact when she heard her describe the little lady with the limp at the beginning of the seance; she herself had often "seen" the ghost with her "psychic eye," and had developed a friendship for her. It was not an unhappy ghost, she contended, and particularly now that her secret was out—why deprive Elizabeth Bullock of "her family"? Why indeed?

The house is still there on Bank Street, and the can of ashes still graces the piano. Whether the E. C. Bullock who called on the Slatins in 1957 was the Eddie whom the ghost claimed as her son, I can't tell. My efforts to locate him in California proved as fruitless as the earlier attempts to locate any other kin.

So the Slatins continue to live happily in their lovely, quiet house in the Village, with Elizabeth Bullock as their star boarder. Though I doubt the census taker will want to register her.

THE
WHISTLING
GHOST

One of my dear friends is the celebrated clairvoyant Florence Sternfels of Edgewater, New Jersey, a lady who has assisted many a police department in the apprehension of criminals or lost persons. Her real ambition, however, is to assist serious scientists to find out what makes her "different," where that power she has— "the forces," as she calls them—comes from. Many times in the past she had *volunteered* her time to sit with investigators, something few professional mediums will do.

I had not seen Florence in over a year when one day the telephone rang, and her slightly creaky voice wished me a cheery hello. It seemed that a highly respected psychiatrist in nearby Croton, New York, had decided to experiment with Florence's psychic powers. Would I come along? She wanted me there to make sure "everything was on the up-and-up." I agreed to come, and the following day Dr. Kahn himself called me, and arrangements were made for a young couple, the Hendersons, to pick me up in their car and drive me out to Croton.

When we arrived at the sumptuous Kahn house near the Hudson River, some thirty persons, mostly neighbors and friends of the doctor's, had already assembled. None of them was known to Florence, of course, and few knew anything about the purpose of her visit. But the doctor was such a well-known community leader and teacher that they had come in great expectations.

The house was a remodeled older house, with an upstairs, and a large garden going all the way down to the river.

Florence did not disappoint the good doctor. Seated at the head of an oval, next to me, she rapidly called out facts and names about people in the room, their relatives and friends, deceased or otherwise, and found quick response and acknowledgment. Startling information, like "a five-year-old child has died, and the mother, who is paralyzed in the legs, is present." She certainly was. "Anyone here lost a collie dog?" Yes, someone had, three weeks before. Florence was a big success.

When it was all over, the crowd broke up and I had a chance to talk to our hostess, the doctor's young wife. She seemed deeply interested in psychic matters, just as was her husband; but while it was strictly a scientific curiosity with Dr. Kahn, his wife seemed to be intuitive and was given to "impressions" herself.

"*You know, I think we've got a ghost,*" she said, looking at me as if she had just said the most ordinary thing in the world.

We walked over to a quiet corner, and I asked her what were her reasons for this extraordinary statement—unusual for the wife of a prominent psychiatrist. She assured me it was no hallucination.

"He's a whistling ghost," she confided, "always whistling the same song, about four bars of it—a happy tune. I guess he must be a happy ghost!"

"When did all this start?" I asked.

"During the past five years I've heard him about twenty times," Mrs. Kahn replied. "Always the same tune."

"And your husband, does he hear it, too?"

She shook her head.

"But he hears raps. Usually in our bedroom, and late at night. They always come in threes. My husband hears it, gets up, and asks who is it, but of course there is nobody there, so he gets no answer.

"Last winter, around three in the morning, we were awakened by a heavy knocking sound on the front door. When we got to the door and opened it, there was no one in sight. The path leading up to the road was empty, too, and believe me, no one could have come down that path and not be still visible by the time we got to the door!"

"And the whistling—where do you hear it usually?"

"Always in the living room—here," Mrs. Kahn replied, pointing at the high-ceilinged, wood-paneled room, with its glass wall facing the garden.

"You see, this living room used to be a stage . . . the house was once a summer theater, and we reconverted the stage area into this room. Come to think of it, I also heard that whistling in the bedroom that was used by the former owner of the house, the man who built both the theater and the house."

"What about this man? Who was he?"

"Clifford Harmon. He was murdered by the Nazis during World War II, when he got trapped in France. The house is quite old, has many secret passageways—as a matter of fact, only three weeks ago, I dreamed I should enter one of the passages!"

"You dreamed this?" I said. "Did anything ever come of it, though?"

Mrs. Kahn nodded. "The next morning, I decided to do just what I had done in my dream during the night. I entered the passage I had seen myself enter in the dream, and then I came across some musty old photographs."

I looked at the pictures. They showed various actors of both sexes, in the costumes of an earlier period. Who knows what personal tragedy or joy the people in these photographs had experienced in this very room? I returned the stack of pictures to Mrs. Kahn.

"Are you mediumistic?" I asked Mrs. Kahn. It seemed to me that she was the catalyst in this house.

"Well, perhaps a little. I am certainly clairvoyant. Some time ago, I wrote to my parents in Miami, and for some unknown reason, addressed the letter to 3251 South 23rd Lane. There was no such address as far as I knew, and the letter was returned to me in a few days. Later, my parents wrote to me telling me they had just bought a house at 3251 South 23rd Lane."

At this point, the doctor joined the conversation, and we talked about Harmon.

"He's left much unfinished business over here, I'm sure," the doctor said. "He had big plans for building and improvements of his property, and, of course, there were a number of girls he was interested in."

I had heard enough. The classic pattern of the haunted house was all there. The ghost, the unfinished business, the willing owners. I offered to hold a "rescue circle" type of seance, to make contact with the "whistling ghost."

We decided to hold the seance on August 3rd, 1960, and that I would bring along Mrs. Meyers, since this called for a trance medium, while Florence, who had originally brought me to this house, was a clairvoyant and psychometrist. A psychometrist gets "impressions" by holding objects that belong to a certain person.

Again, the transportation was provided by Mrs. Henderson, whose husband could not come along this time. On this occasion there was no curious crowd in the large living room when we arrived. Only the house guests of the Kahns, consisting of a Mr. and Mrs. Bower and their daughter, augmented the circle we formed as soon as the doctor had arrived from a late call. As always, before sliding into trance, Mrs. Meyers gave us her psychic impressions; before going into the full trance it is necessary to make the desired contact.

"Some names," said Mrs. Meyers, "a Robert, a Delia, a Harold and the name Banks . . . Oh . . . and then a Hart." She seemed unsure of the proper spelling.

At this very moment, both Mrs. Kahn and I distinctly heard the sound of heavy breathing. It seemed to emanate from somewhere above and behind the sitters. "Melish and Goldfarb!" Mrs. Meyers mumbled, getting more and more into a somnambulant state. "That's strange!" Dr. Kahn interjected. "There was a man named Elish here, some fifteen years ago . . . and a Mr. Goldwag, recently!"

"Mary . . . something—Ann," the medium now said. Later, after the seance, Dr. Kahn told me that Harmon's private secretary, who had had full charge of the big estate, was a woman named—Mary Brasnahan. . . .

Now Mrs. Meyers described a broad-shouldered man with iron-gray hair, who, she said, became gray at a very early age. "He wears a double-breasted, dark blue coat, and has a tiny mustache. His initials are R. H." Then she added, "I see handwriting . . . papers . . . signatures . . . and there is another, younger man, smaller, with light brown hair—and he is concerned with some papers that belong in files. His initials are J. B. I think the first man is the boss, this one is the clerk." Then she added suddenly, "Deborah!"

At this point Mrs. Meyers herself pulled back, and said: "I feel a twitch in my arm; apparently this isn't for publication!" But she continued and described other people whom she "felt" around the house; a Gertrude, for instance, and a bald-headed man with a reddish complexion, rather stout, whom she called B. B. "He has to do with the settlements on Deborah and the other girls."

Mrs. Meyers knew of course nothing about Harmon's alleged reputation as a bit of a ladies' man.

"That's funny," she suddenly commented, "I see two women dressed in very old-fashioned clothes, much earlier than their own period."

I had not mentioned a word to Mrs. Meyers about the theatrical usage which the house had once been put to. Evidently she received the impressions of two actresses.

"Bob . . . he's being called by a woman."

At this point, full trance set in, and the medium's own personality vanished, to allow the ghost to speak to us directly, if he so chose. After a moment Albert, the medium's control, came and announced that the ghost would speak to us. Then he withdrew, and within seconds a strange face replaced the usual benign expression of Mrs. Meyer's face. This was a shrewd, yet dignified man. His voice, at first faint, grew in strength as the seconds ticked off.

"So . . . so it goes . . . Sing a Song of Sixpence . . . all over now. . . ."

Excitedly Mrs. Kahn grabbed my arm and whispered into my ear: "That's the name of the song *he* always whistled . . . I couldn't think of it before." Through my mind went the words of the old nursery rhyme—

Sing a Song of Sixpence,
A pocket full of rye,

Four and Twenty Blackbirds,
Baked in a pie.
When the pie was opened,
The birds began to sing
Isn't that a dainty dish
To set before the King?

Like a wartime password, our ghost had identified himself through the medium.

Why did Harmon pick this song as his tune? Perhaps the gay lilt, the carefree air that goes with it, perhaps a sentimental reason. Mrs. Kahn was aglow with excitement.

The communicator then continued to speak: "All right, he won't come anymore. She isn't here . . . when you're dead, you're alive."

I thought it was time to ask a few questions of my own. "Why are you here?"

"Pleasant and unpleasant memories. My own thoughts keep me . . . happy, loved her. One happiness—*he* stands in the way. She didn't get what was hers. Jimmy may get it for her. *He* stands in the way!"

"Why do you come to this house?"

"To meet with her. It was our meeting place in the flesh. We still commune in spirit though she's still with you, and I return. We can meet. It is my house. My thought-child."

What he was trying to say, I thought, is that in her dream state, she has contact with him. Most unusual, even for a ghost! I began to wonder who "she" was. It was worth a try.

"Is her name Deborah?" I ventured. But the reaction was so violent our ghost slipped away. Albert took over the medium and requested that no more painfully personal questions be asked of the ghost. He also explained that our friend was indeed the owner of the house, the other man seen by the medium, his secretary, but the raps the doctor had heard had been caused by another person, the man who is after the owner's lady love.

Presently the ghost returned, and confirmed this.

"I whistle to call her. He does the rappings, to rob. . . ."

"Is there any unfinished business you want to tell us about?" That should not be too personal, I figured.

"None worth returning for, only love."

"Is there anything under the house?" I wondered. . . .

"There is a small tunnel, but it is depleted now." At this, I looked searchingly toward the doctor, who nodded, and later told me that such a tunnel did indeed exist.

"What is your name?"

"Bob. I only whistle and sing for happiness."

Before I could question him further, the gentleman slipped out again, and once more Albert, the control, took over:

"This man died violently at the hands of a firing squad," he commented, "near a place he thinks is Austerlitz . . . but is not sure. As for the estate, the other woman had the larger share."

There was nothing more after that, so I requested that the seance be concluded.

After the medium had returned to her own body, we

discussed the experience, and Dr. Kahn remarked that he was not sure about the name Harmon had used among his friends. It seemed absurd to think that Clifford, his official first name, would not be followed by something more familiar—like, for instance, Bob. But there was no certainty.

"Did the Nazis really kill him?" I asked. There was total silence in the big room now. You could have heard a pin drop, and the Bowers, who had never been to any seances before, just sat there with their hands at their chins, wide-eyed and full of excitement. Albert, through his "instrument," as he called his medium, took his time to answer me.

"I'm afraid so. But I don't think it was a firing squad that killed him. He was beaten to death!" I looked with horror at Dr. Kahn, trying to get confirmation, but he only shrugged his shoulders.

Actually, nobody knows exactly how Harmon died, he revealed later. The fact is that the Nazis murdered him during the war. Could he have meant *Auschwitz* instead of Austerlitz?

I didn't feel like pursuing the subject any further. With Albert's assistance, we ended the seance, bringing the medium out of her trance state as quickly as possible.

The lights, which had been subdued during the sitting, were now allowed to be turned back on again. Mrs. Meyers recalled very little of what had transpired, mostly events and phrases at the onset and very end of her trance condition, but nothing that happened in the middle portion, when her trance state was at its deepest.

It was now midnight, and time to return to New York. As I said good night to my mediumistic friend, I expressed my hope that all would now be quiet at Croton.

This was wishful thinking.

The following morning, Mrs. Kahn telephoned me long distance. Far from being quiet—the manifestations had increased around the house.

"What exactly happened?" I inquired. Mrs. Kahn bubbled over with excitement.

"We went to bed shortly after you left," she replied, "and all seemed so peaceful. Then, at 3:00 A.M., suddenly the bedroom lights went on by themselves. There is only one switch. Neither my husband nor I had gotten out of bed to turn on that switch. Nevertheless, when I took a look at the switch, it was *turned down,* as if by human hands!"

"Amazing," I conceded.

"Oh, but that isn't all," she continued. "Exactly one hour later, at four o'clock, the same thing happened again. By the way, do you remember the drapery covering the bedroom wall? There isn't a door or window nearby. Besides, they were all shut. No possible air current could have moved those draperies. All the same, I saw the draperies move by their own accord, plainly and visibly."

"I suppose he wants to let you know he's still there!" I said, rather meekly. Ghosts can be persistent at times. But Mrs. Kahn had more to tell me.

"Our house guest, Mrs. Bower, has the room that used to be Harmon's bedroom. Well, this morning she was dressing in front of the big closet. Suddenly she saw the door to the room open slowly, and then, with enormous force, pin her into the closet! There was nobody outside the room, of course."

"Anything else?" I asked quietly.

"Not really. Only, I had a dream last night. It was about a man in a blue suit. You remember Mrs. Meyers saw a man in a blue suit, too. Only with me, he said, 'Miller.' Said it several times, to make sure I got it. I also dreamed of a woman in a blue dress, with two small children, who was in danger somehow. But Miller stood out the strongest."

I thanked Mrs. Kahn for her report, and made her promise me to call me the instant there were any further disturbances.

I woke up the following morning, sure the phone would ring and Mrs. Kahn would have more to tell me. But I was wrong. All remained quiet. All remained peaceful the next morning, too. It was not until four days later that Mrs. Kahn called again.

I prepared myself for some more of the ghost's shenanigans. But, to my relief, Mrs. Kahn called to tell me no further manifestations had occurred. However, she had done a bit of investigating. Since the name "Miller" was totally unknown to her and the doctor, she inquired around the neighborhood. Finally, one of the neighbors did recall a Miller. He was Harmon's personal physician.

"One thing I forgot to mention while you were here," she added. "Harmon's bed was stored away for many years. I decided one day to use it again. One night my husband discovered nails similar to carpet tacks under the pillow. We were greatly puzzled—but for lack of an explanation, we just forgot the incident. Another time I found something similar to crushed glass in the bed, and again, although greatly puzzled—forgot the incident. I don't know whether or not these seemingly unexplainable incidents mean anything."

Could it be that Harmon objected to anyone else using his bed? Ghosts are known to be quite possessive of their earthly goods, and resentful of "intruders."

All seemed quiet at the Kahns, until I received another call from Mrs. Kahn the last days of October.

The "Whistling Ghost" was back.

This was quite a blow to my prestige as a ghost hunter, but on the other hand, Harmon's wraith apparently was a happy spirit and liked being earthbound. To paraphrase a well-known expression, you can lead a ghost to the spirit world, but you can't make him stay—if he doesn't want to. Next morning a note came from Mrs. Kahn.

"As I told you via phone earlier this evening, we again heard our whistler last night about 1:00 A.M., and it was the loudest I have ever heard. I didn't have to strain for it. My husband heard it too, but he thought it was the wind in the chimney. Then, as it continued, he agreed that it was some sort of phenomena. I got out of bed and went toward the sound of the whistle. I reached the den, from where I could see into the living room. Light was coming through a window behind me and was reflected upon the ceiling of the living room . . . *I saw a small white mist,* floating, but motionless, in front of the table in the living room. I called to my husband. He looked, but saw nothing. He said he would put the light on and I watched him *walk right through the mist*—he turned the lamp on and everything returned to normal."

I haven't spoken with the Kahns in several months now.

Is the whistling ghost still around? If he is, nobody seems to mind. That's how it is sometimes with happy ghosts. They get to be one of the family.

THE
METUCHEN
GHOST

O ne day last spring, while the snow was still on the
ground and the chill in the air, my good friend
Bernard Axelrod, with whom I have shared many
a ghostly experience, called to say that he knew of a haunted
house in New Jersey, and was I still interested.

I was, and Bernard disclosed that in the little town of
Metuchen, there were a number of structures dating back to
Colonial days. A few streets down from where he and his
family live in a modern, up-to-date brick building, there
stands one wooden house in particular which has the reputation of being haunted, Bernard explained. No particulars
were known to him beyond that. Ever since the Rockland
County Ghost in the late Danton Walker's colonial house
had acquainted me with the specters from George Washington's days, I have been eager to enlarge this knowledge. So it

was with great anticipation that I gathered a group of help-
ers to pay a visit to whoever might be haunting the house in
Metuchen. Bernard, who is a very persuasive fellow, managed to get permission from the owner of the house, Mr.
Kane, an advertising executive. My group included Mrs.
Meyers, as medium, and two associates of hers who would
operate the tape recorder and take notes, Rosemarie de Simone and Pearl Winder. Miss de Simone is a teacher and Mrs.
Winder is the wife of a dentist.

It was midafternoon of March 6, 1960, when we rolled
into the sleepy town of Metuchen. Bernard Axelrod was
expecting us, and took us across town to the colonial house
we were to inspect.

Any mention of the history or background of the house
was studiously avoided en route. The owners, Mr. and Mrs.
Kane, had a guest, a Mr. David, and the eight of us sat down
in a circle in the downstairs living room of the beautifully
preserved old house. It is a jewel of a colonial country house,
with an upper story, a staircase and very few structural
changes. No doubt about it, the Kanes had good taste, and
their house reflected it. The furniture was all in the style
of the period, which I took to be about the turn of the
eighteenth century, perhaps earlier. There were several cats
smoothly moving about, which helped me greatly to relax,
for I have always felt that no house is wholly bad where there
are cats, and conversely, where there are several cats, a house
is bound to be wonderfully charming. For the occasion,
however, the entire feline menagerie was put out of reach
into the kitchen, and the tape recorder turned on as we took

our seats in a semicircle around the fireplace. The light was the subdued light of a late winter afternoon, and the quiet was that of a country house far away from the bustling city. It was a perfect setting for a ghost to have his say.

As Mrs. Meyers eased herself into her comfortable chair, she remarked that certain clairvoyant impressions had come to her almost the instant she set foot into the house.

"I met a woman upstairs—in spirit, that is—with a long face, thick cheeks, perhaps forty years old or more, with ash-brown hair that may once have been blond. Somehow I get the name Mathilda. She wears a dress of striped material down to her knees, then wide plain material to her ankles. She puts out a hand, and I see a heavy wedding band on her finger, *but it has a cut in it,* and she insists on calling my attention to the cut. Then there is a man, with a prominent nose, tan coat and black trousers, standing in the back of the room looking as if he were sorry about something . . . he has very piercing eyes . . . I think she'd like to find something she has lost, and he blames her for it."

We were listening attentively. No one spoke, for that would perhaps give Mrs. Meyers an unconscious lead, something a good researcher will avoid.

"That sounds very interesting," I heard Bernard say, in his usual noncommittal way. "Do you see anything else?"

"Oh, yes," Mrs. Meyers nodded, "quite a bit—for one thing, there are *other* people here who don't belong to *them* at all . . . they come with the place, but in a different period . . . funny, halfway between upstairs and downstairs, I see one or two people *hanging.*"

At this remark, the Kanes exchanged quick glances. Evidently my medium had hit pay dirt. Later, Mr. Kane told us a man committed suicide in the house around 1850 or 1860. He confirmed also that there was once a floor in between the two floors, but that this later addition had since been removed, when the house was restored to its original colonial condition.

Built in 1740, the house had replaced an earlier structure, for objects inscribed "1738" have been unearthed here.

"Legend has always had it that a revolutionary soldier haunts the house," Mr. Kane explained after the seance. "The previous owners told us they did hear *peculiar noises* from time to time, and that they had been told of such goings-on also by the owner who preceded *them*. Perhaps this story has been handed down from owner to owner, but we have never spoken to anyone in our generation who has heard or seen anything unusual about the place."

"What about you and your wife?" I inquired.

"Oh, we were a bit luckier—or unluckier—depending on how you look at it. One day back in 1956, the front door knocker banged away very loudly. My wife, who was all alone in the house at the time, went to see who it was. There was nobody there. It was winter, and deep snow surrounded the house. *There were no tracks in the snow.*"

"How interesting," Bernard said. All this was new to him, too, despite his friendship with the family.

Mr. Kane slowly lit a pipe, blew the smoke toward the low ceiling of the room, and continued.

"The previous owners had a dog. Big, strapping fellow.

Just the same, now and again he would hear some strange noises and absolutely panic. In the middle of the night he would jump into bed with them, crazed with fear. But it wasn't just the dog who heard things. They, too, heard the walking—steps of someone walking around the second floor, and in their bedroom, on the south side of the house—at times of the day when they *knew* for sure there was nobody there."

"And after you moved in, did you actually *see* anything?" I asked. Did they have any idea what the ghost looked like?

"Well, yes," Mr. Kane said. "About a year ago, Mrs. Kane was sleeping in the Green Room upstairs. *Three nights in a row, she was awakened in the middle of the night, at the same time, by the feeling of a presence.* Looking up, she noticed a white form standing beside her bed. Thinking it was me, at first, she was not frightened. But when she spoke to it, it just disappeared into air. She is sure it was a man."

Although nothing unusual had occurred since, the uncanny feeling persisted, and when Bernard Axelrod mentioned his interest in ghosts, and offered to have me come to the house with a qualified medium, the offer was gladly accepted. So there we were, with Mrs. Meyers slowly gliding into trance. Gradually, her description of what she saw or heard blended into the personalities themselves, as her own personality vanished temporarily. It was a very gradual transition, and well controlled.

"She is being blamed by him," Mrs. Meyers mumbled. "Now I see a table, she took four mugs, four large mugs, and one small one. Does she mean to say, four older people and a small one? I get a name, Jake, John, no, *Jonathan*! Then there are four Indians, and they want to make peace. *They've done something they should not have,* and they want to make peace." Her visions continued.

"Now instead of the four mugs on the table, there's a whole line of them, fifteen altogether, but I don't see the small mug now. There are many individuals standing around the table, with their backs toward me—then someone is calling and screaming, and someone says 'Off above the knees.'"

I later established through research that during the Revolutionary War the house was right in the middle of many small skirmishes; the injured may well have been brought here for treatment.

Mrs. Meyers continued her narrative with increasing excitement in her voice.

"Now there are other men, all standing there with long-tailed coats, white stockings, and talking. Someone says 'Dan Dayridge' or 'Bainbridge,' I can't make it out clearly; he's someone with one of these three-cornered hats, a white wig, tied black hair, a very thin man with a high, small nose, not particularly young, with a fluffy collar and large eyes. Something took place here in which he was a participant. He is one of the men standing there with those fifteen mugs. It is night, and there are two candles on either side of the table, food on the table—*smells like chicken*—and then there is a paper with red seals and gold ribbon. But something goes wrong with this, and now there are only four mugs on the table . . . I think it means, only four men return. *Not the small one.* This man is one of the four, and somehow the little mug is pushed aside, I see it put away on the shelf. I see now a small boy, he has disappeared, he is gone . . . but always trying to *come back*. The name *Allen* . . . he followed the man, but the Indians got him and he never came back. They're looking for him, trying to find him. . . ."

Mrs. Meyers now seemed totally entranced. Her features assumed the face of a woman in great mental anguish, and her voice quivered; the words came haltingly and with much prodding from me. For all practical purposes, the medium had now been taken over by a troubled spirit. We listened quietly, as the story unfolded.

"*Allen's* coming back one day . . . call him back . . . my son, do you hear him? They put those Indians in the tree, do you hear them as they moan?"

"Who took your boy?" I asked gently.

"They did . . . he went with them, with the men. With his father, *Jon.*"

"What Indians took him?"

"Look there in the tree. They didn't do it. I know they didn't do it."

"Where did they go?"

"To the *river.* My boy, did you hear him?"

Mrs. Meyers could not have possibly known that there was a river not far from the house. I wanted to fix the period of our story, as I always do in such cases, so I interrupted the narrative and asked what day this was. There was a brief pause, as if she were collecting her thoughts. Then the faltering voice was heard again.

"December One...."

December One! The old-fashioned way of saying December First.

"What year is this?" I continued.

This time the voice seemed puzzled as to why I would ask such an obvious thing, but she obliged.

"Seventeen ... seventy ... six."

"What does your husband do?"

"Jonathan ...?"

"Does he own property?"

"The field...."

But then the memory of her son returned. "Allen, my son Allen. He is calling me....

"Where was he born?"

"Here."

"What is the name of this town?"

"Bayridge."

Subsequently, I found that the section of Metuchen we were in had been known in colonial times as *Woodbridge*, although it is not inconceivable that there also was a Bayridge.

The woman wanted to pour her heart out now. "Oh, look," she continued, "they didn't do it, they're in the tree ... those Indians, dead ones. They didn't do it, I can see their souls and they were innocent of this ... in the cherry tree."

Suddenly she interrupted herself and said—"Where am I? Why am I so sad?"

It isn't uncommon for a newly liberated or newly contacted "ghost" to be confused about his or her own status. Only an emotionally disturbed personality becomes an earthbound "ghost."

I continued the questioning.

Between sobs and cries for her son, Allen, she let the name "Mary Dugan" slip from her lips, or rather the lips of the entranced medium, who now was fully under the unhappy one's control.

"Who is Mary Dugan?" I immediately interrupted.

"He married her, Jonathan."

"Second wife?"

"Yes . . . I am under the tree."

"Where were you born? What was your maiden name?"

"Bayridge . . . Swift . . . my heart is so hurt, so cold, so cold."

"Do you have any other children?"

"Allen . . . Mary Anne . . . Georgia. They're calling me, do you hear them? Allen, he knows I am alone waiting here. He thought he was a *man*!"

"How old was your boy at the time?" I said. The disappearance of her son was the one thing foremost in her mind.

"My boy . . . eleven . . . December One, 1776, is his birthday. That was his birthday all right."

I asked her if Allen had another name, and she said, Peter. Her own maiden name? She could not remember.

"Why don't I know? They threw me out . . . it was Mary took the house."

"What did your husband do?"

"He was a *potter*. He also was paid for harness. His shop . . . the road to the south. Bayridge. In the tree orchard we took from two neighbors."

The neighborhood is known for its clay deposits and potters, but this was as unknown to the medium as it was to me until *after* the seance, when Bernard told us about it.

In *Boyhood Days in Old Metuchen,* a rare work, Dr. David Marshall says: "Just south of Metuchen there are extensive clay banks."

But our visitor had enough of the questioning. Her sorrow returned and suddenly she burst into tears, the medium's tears, to be sure, crying—"I want Allen! Why is it I look for him? I hear him calling me, I hear his step . . . I know he is here . . . why am I searching for him?"

I then explained that Allen was on "her side of the veil," too, that she would be reunited with her boy by merely "standing still" and letting him find her; it was her frantic activity that made it impossible for them to be reunited, but if she were to becalm herself, all would be well.

After a quiet moment of reflection, her sobs became weaker and her voice firmer.

"Can you see your son now?"

"Yes, I see him." And with that, she slipped away quietly.

A moment later, the medium returned to her own body, as it were, and rubbed her sleepy eyes. Fully awakened a moment later, she remembered nothing of the trance. Now *for the first time* did we talk about the house, and its ghostly visitors.

"How much of this can be proved?" I asked impatiently.

Mr. Kane lit another pipe, and then answered me slowly.

"Well, there is quite a lot," he finally said. "For one thing, this house used to be a tavern during revolutionary days, known as the Allen House!"

Bernard Axelrod, a few weeks later, discovered an 1870 history of the town of Metuchen. In it, there was a remark anent the house, which an early map showed at its present site in 1799:

"In the house . . . lived a Mrs. Allen, and on it was a sign 'Allentown Cake and Beer Sold Here.' Between the long Prayer Meetings which according to New England custom were held mornings and afternoons, with half hour or an hour intermission, it was not unusual for the young men to get ginger cake and a glass of beer at this famous restaurant. . . ."

"What about all those Indians she mentioned?" I asked Mr. Kane.

"There were Indians in this region all right," he confirmed.

"Indian arrowheads have been found right here, near the pond in back of the house. Many Indian battles were fought around here, and incidentally, during the War for Independence, both sides came to this house and had their ale in the evening. This was a kind of no-man's land between the Americans and the British. During the day, they would kill each other, but at night, *they ignored each other over a beer at Mrs. Allen's tavern!*"

"How did you get this information?" I asked Mr. Kane.

"There was a local historian, a Mr. Welsh, who owned this house for some thirty years. He also talked of a revolutionary soldier whose ghost was seen plainly 'walking' through the house about a foot off the ground."

Many times have I heard a ghostly apparition described in just such terms. The motion of walking is really unnecessary, it seems, for the spirit form *glides* about a place.

There are interesting accounts in the rare old books about the town of Metuchen in the local library. These stories spoke of battles between the British and Americans, and of "carts loaded with dead bodies, after a battle between British soldiers and Continentals, up around Oak Tree on June 26th, 1777."

No doubt, the Allen House saw many of them brought in along with the wounded and dying.

I was particularly interested in finding proof of Jonathan Allen's existence, and details of his life.

So far I had only ascertained that Mrs. Allen existed. Her husband was my next goal.

After much work, going through old wills and land documents, I discovered a number of Allens in the area. I found the will of his father, Henry, leaving his "son, Jonathan, the land where he lives" on April 4th, 1783.

A 1799 map shows a substantial amount of land marked

"Land of Allen," and Jonathan Allen's name occurs in many a document of the period as a witness or seller of land.

The Jonathan Allen I wanted had to be from Middlesex County, in which Metuchen was located. I recalled that he was an able-bodied man, and consequently must have seen some service. Sure enough, in the *Official Register of the Officers and Men of New Jersey in the Revolutionary War,* I found my man—"Allen, Jonathan—Middlesex."

It is good to know that the troubled spirit of Mrs. Allen can now rest close to her son's; and perhaps the other restless one, her husband, will be accused of negligence in the boy's death no more.

THE STRANGER
AT THE DOOR

I have found that there are ghosts in all sorts of places, in ancient castles, modern apartment houses, farms and ships—but it is somewhat of a jolt to find out you've lived in a house for a few years and didn't even know it was haunted. But that is exactly what happened to me.

For three years I was a resident of a beautiful twenty-nine-story apartment building on Riverside Drive. I lived on the nineteenth floor, and seldom worried about what transpired below me. But I was aware of the existence of a theater and a museum on the ground floor of the building. I was also keenly aware of numerous inspired paintings, some Tibetan, some Occidental, adorning the corridors of this building. The museum is nowadays known as the Riverside Museum, and the paintings were largely the work of the great Roerich, a painter who sought his inspirations mainly in the mysticism of Tibet, where he spent many years. On his return from the East, his many admirers decided to chip in a few millions and build him a monument worthy of his name. Thus, in 1930, was raised the Rohrach building as a center of the then flourishing cult of Eastern mysticism, of which Rohrach was the high priest. After his death, a schism appeared among his followers, and an exodus took place. A new "Roerich Museum" (on 107th St.) was established by Seena Fosdick, and is still in existence a few blocks away from the imposing twenty-nine-story structure originally known by that name. In turn, the building where I lived changed its name to that of the Master Institute, a combination apartment building and school, and, of course, art gallery.

It was in February of 1960 when I met at a tea party—yes, there are such things in this day and age—a young actress and producer, Mrs. Roland, who had an interesting experience at "my" building some years ago. She was not sure whether it was 1952 or 1953, but she was quite sure that it happened exactly the way she told it to me that winter afternoon in the apartment of famed author Claudia de Lys.

A lecture-meeting dealing with Eastern philosophy had drawn her to the Roerich building. Ralph Huston, the eminent philosopher, presided over the affair, and a full turnout it was. As the speaker held the attention of the crowd, Mrs. Roland's eyes wandered off to the rear of the room. Her interest was invited by a tall stranger standing near the door, listening quietly and with rapt attention. Mrs. Roland didn't know too many of the active members, and the stranger, whom she had never seen before, fascinated her. His dress, for one thing, was most peculiar. He wore a gray cotton robe with a high-necked collar, the kind one sees in Oriental paintings, and on his head he had a round black cap. He appeared to be a fairly young man, certainly in the prime of life, and his very dark eyes in particular attracted her.

For a moment she turned her attention to the speaker; when she returned to the door, the young man was gone.

"Peculiar," she thought; "why should he leave in the middle of the lecture? He seemed so interested in it all."

As the devotees of mysticism slowly filed out of the room, the actress sauntered over to Mrs. Fosdick whom she knew to be the "boss lady" of the group.

"Tell me," she inquired, "who was that handsome dark-eyed young man at the door?"

Mrs. Fosdick was puzzled. She did not recall any such person. The actress then described the stranger in every detail. When she had finished, Mrs. Fosdick seemed a bit pale.

But this was an esoteric forum, so she did not hesitate to tell Mrs. Roland that she had apparently seen an apparition. What was more, the description fitted the great Roerich—in his earlier years—to a T. Mrs. Roland had never seen Roerich in the flesh.

At this point, Mrs. Roland confessed that she had psychic abilities, and was often given to "hunches." There was much head shaking, followed by some hand shaking, and then the matter was forgotten.

I was of course interested, for what would be nicer than to have a house ghost, so to speak?

The next morning, I contacted Mrs. Fosdick. Unfortunately, this was one of the occasions when truth did not conquer. When I had finished telling her what I wanted her to confirm, she tightened up, especially when she found out I was living at the "enemy camp," so to speak. Emphatically, Mrs. Fosdick denied the incident, but admitted knowing Mrs. Roland.

With this, I returned to my informant, who reaffirmed the entire matter. Again I approached Mrs. Fosdick with the courage of an unwelcome suitor advancing on the castle of his beloved, fully aware of the dragons lurking in the moat.

While I explained my scientific reasons for wanting her to remember the incident, she launched into a tirade concerning her withdrawal from the "original" Roerich group, which was fascinating, but not to me.

I have no reason to doubt Mrs. Roland's account especially as I found her extremely well poised, balanced, and indeed, psychic.

I only wondered if Mr. Roerich would sometime honor me with a visit, or vice versa, now that we were neighbors?

A GREENWICH VILLAGE GHOST

Back in 1953, when I spent much of my time writing and editing material of a most mundane nature, always, of course, with a weather eye cocked for a good case of hunting, I picked up a copy of *Park East* and found to my amazement some very palatable grist for my psychic mills. "The Ghost of Tenth Street," by Elizabeth Archer, was a well-documented report of the hauntings on that celebrated Greenwich Village street where artists make their headquarters, and many buildings date back to the eighteenth century. Miss Archer's story was later reprinted by *Tomorrow* magazine, upon my suggestion. In *Park East*, some very good illustrations accompany the text, for which there was no room in *Tomorrow*.

Up to 1956, the ancient studio building at 51 West 10th Street was a landmark known to many connoisseurs of old

New York, but it was demolished to make way for one of those nondescript, modern apartment buildings that are gradually taking away the charm of Greenwich Village, and give us doubtful comforts in its stead.

Until the very last, reports of an apparition, allegedly the ghost of artist John La Farge, who died in 1910, continued to come in. A few houses down the street is the Church of the Ascension; the altar painting, "The Ascension," is the work of John La Farge. Actually, the artist did the work on the huge painting at his studio, No. 22, in 51 West 10th Street. He finished it, however, in the church itself, "in place." Having just returned from the Orient, La Farge used a new technique involving the use of several coats of paint, thus making the painting heavier than expected. The painting was hung, but the chassis collapsed; La Farge built a stronger chassis and the painting stayed in place this time. Years went by. Oliver La Farge, the great novelist and grandson of the painter, had spent much of his youth with his celebrated grandfather. One day, while working across the street, he was told the painting had fallen again. Dashing across the street, he found that the painting had indeed fallen, and that his grandfather had died *that very instant*!

The fall of the heavy painting was no trifling matter to La Farge, who was equally as well known as an architect as he was a painter. Many buildings in New York for which he drew the plans seventy-five years ago are still standing. But the construction of the chassis of the altar painting may have been faulty. And therein lies the cause for La Farge's ghostly visitations, it would seem. The artists at No. 51 insisted always that La Farge could not find rest until he had corrected his calculations, searching for the original plans of the chassis to find out what was wrong. An obsession to redeem himself as an artist and craftsman, then, would be the underlying cause for the persistence with which La Farge's ghost returned to his old haunts.

The first such return was reported in 1944, when a painter by the name of Feodor Rimsky and his wife lived in No. 22. Late one evening, they returned from the opera. On approaching their studio, they noticed that a light was on and the door open, although they distinctly remembered having *left it shut*. Rimsky walked into the studio, pushed aside the heavy draperies at the entrance to the studio itself, and stopped in amazement. In the middle of the room, a single lamp plainly revealed a stranger behind the large chair in what Rimsky called his library corner; the man wore a tall black hat and a dark, billowing velvet coat. Rimsky quickly told his wife to wait, and rushed across the room to get a closer look at the intruder. But the man *just vanished* as the painter reached the chair.

Later, Rimsky told of his experience to a former owner of the building, who happened to be an amateur historian. He showed Rimsky some pictures of former tenants of his building. In two of them, Rimsky easily recognized his visitor, wearing exactly the same clothes Rimsky had seen him in. Having come from Europe but recently, Rimsky knew nothing of La Farge and had never seen a picture of him. The ball dress worn by the ghost had not been common at the turn of the century, but La Farge was known to affect such strange attire.

Three years later, the Rimskys were entertaining some guests at their studio, including an advertising man named William Weber, who was known to have had psychic experiences in the past. But Weber never wanted to discuss this "special talent" of his, for fear of being ridiculed. As the conversation flowed among Weber, Mrs. Weber, and two other guests, the advertising man's wife noticed her husband's sudden stare at a cabinet on the other side of the room, where paintings were stored. She saw nothing, but Weber asked her in an excited tone of voice—"Do you see that man in the cloak and top hat over there?"

Weber knew nothing of the ghostly tradition of the studio or of John La Farge; no stranger could have gotten by the door without being noticed, and none had been expected at this hour. The studio was locked from the *inside*.

After that, the ghost of John La Farge was heard many times by a variety of tenants at No. 51, opening windows or pushing draperies aside, but not until 1948 was he *seen* again.

Up a flight of stairs from Studio 22, but connected to it—artists like to visit each other—was the studio of illustrator John Alan Maxwell. Connecting stairs and a "secret rest room" used by La Farge had long been walled up in the many structural changes in the old building. Only the window of the walled-up room was still visible from the outside. It was in this area that Rimsky felt that the restless spirit of John La Farge was trapped. As Miss Archer puts it in her narrative, "walled in like the Golem, sleeping through the day and close to the premises for roaming through the night."

After many an unsuccessful search of Rimsky's studio, apparently the ghost started to look in Maxwell's studio. In the spring of 1948, the ghost of La Farge made his initial appearance in the illustrator's studio.

It was a warm night, and Maxwell had gone to bed naked, pulling the covers over himself. Suddenly he awakened. From the amount of light coming in through the skylight, he judged the time to be about one or two in the morning. *He had the uncanny feeling of not being alone in the room.* As his eyes got used to the darkness, he clearly distinguished the figure of a tall woman, bending over his bed, lifting and straightening his sheets several times over. Behind her, there was a man staring at a wooden filing cabinet at the foot of the couch. Then he opened a drawer, looked in it, and closed it again. Getting hold of himself, Maxwell noticed that the woman wore a light red dress of the kind worn in the last century, and the man a white shirt and dark cravat of the same period. It never occurred to the illustrator that they were anything but *people*; probably, he thought, models in costume working for one of the artists in the building.

The woman then turned to her companion as if to say something, but did not, and walked off toward the dark room at the other end of the studio. The man then went back to the cabinet and leaned on it, head in hand. By now Maxwell had regained his wits and thought the intruders must be burglars, although he could not figure out how they had entered his place, since he had locked it from the *inside* before going to bed! Making a fist, he struck at the stranger, yelling, "Put your hands up!"

His voice could be heard clearly along the empty corridors. *But his fist went through the man and into the filing cabinet.* Nursing his injured wrist, he realized that his visitors had dissolved into thin air. There was no one in the dark room. The door was still securely locked. The skylight, 150 feet above ground, could not very well have served as an escape route *to anyone human.* By now Maxwell knew that La Farge and his wife had paid him a social call.

Other visitors to No. 51 complained about strange winds and sudden chills when passing La Farge's walled-up room. One night, one of Maxwell's lady visitors returned, shortly after leaving his studio, in great agitation, yelling, "That man! That man!" The inner court of the building was glass-enclosed, so that one could see clearly across to the corridors on the other side of the building. Maxwell and his remaining guests saw nothing there.

But the woman insisted that she saw a strange man under one of the old gaslights in the building; he seemed to lean against the wall of the corridor, dressed in old-fashioned clothes and *possessed of a face so cadaverous and death-mask-like, that it set her ascreaming*!

This was the first time the face of the ghost had been observed clearly by anyone. The sight was enough to make her run back to Maxwell's studio. Nobody could have left without being seen through the glass-enclosed corridors and no one had seen a stranger in the building that evening. As usual, he had vanished into thin air.

So much for Miss Archer's account of the La Farge ghost. My own investigation was sparked by her narrative, and I telephoned her at her Long Island home, inviting her to come along if and when we held a seance at No. 51.

I was then working with a group of parapsychology students meeting at the rooms of the Association for Research and Enlightenment (Cayce Foundation) on West Sixteenth Street. The director of this group was a phototechnician of the *Daily News,* Bernard Axelrod, who was the only one of the group who knew the purpose of the meeting; the others, notably the medium, Mrs. Meyers, knew nothing whatever of our plans.

We met in front of Bigelow's drugstore that cold evening, February 23, 1954, and proceeded to 51 West Tenth Street, where the current occupant of the La Farge studio, an artist named Leon Smith, welcomed us. In addition, there were also present the late *News* columnist, Danton Walker, Henry Belk, the noted playwright Bernays, Marguerite Haymes, and two or three others considered students of psychic phenomena. Unfortunately, Mrs. Belk also brought along her pet chihuahua, which proved to be somewhat of a problem.

All in all, there were fifteen people present in the high-ceilinged, chilly studio. Dim light crept through the tall windows that looked onto the courtyard, and one wished that the fireplace occupying the center of the back wall had been working.

We formed a circle around it, with the medium occupying a comfortable chair directly opposite it, and the sitters filling out the circle on both sides; my own chair was next to the medium's.

The artificial light was dimmed. Mrs. Meyers started to enter the trance state almost immediately and only the loud ticking of the clock in the rear of the room was heard for a while, as her breathing became heavier. At the threshold of passing into trance, the medium suddenly said—

"Someone says very distinctly, *Take another step and I go out this window!* The body of a woman . . . close-fitting hat and a plume . . . close-fitting bodice and a thick skirt . . . lands right on face . . . I see a man, dark curly hair, *hooked nose, an odd, mean face* . . . cleft in chin . . . light tan coat, lighter britches, boots, whip in hand, cruel, mean. . . ."

There was silence as she described *what I recognized as the face of La Farge.*

A moment later she continued: "I know the face is not to be looked at anymore. It is horrible. It should have hurt but I didn't remember. Not long. I just want to scream and scream."

The power of the woman who went through the window was strong. "I have a strange feeling," Mrs. Meyers said, "I *have to go out that window* if I go into trance." With a worried look, she turned to me and asked, "If I stand up and start to move, *hold me.*" I nodded assurance and the seance continued. A humming sound came from her lips, gradually assuming human-voice characteristics.

The next personality to manifest itself was apparently a woman in great fear. "They're in the courtyard.... He is coming ... they'll find me and whip me again. I'll die first. Let me go. I shouldn't talk so loud. Margaret! Please don't let him come. See the child. My child. Barbara. Oh, the steps, I can't take it. Take Bobby, raise her, I can't take it. He is coming ... *let me go!* I am free!"

With this, the medium broke out of trance and complained of facial stiffness, as well as pain in the shoulder.

Was the frantic woman someone who had been mistreated by an early inhabitant of No. 22? Was she a runaway slave, many of whom had found refuge in the old houses and alleys of the Village?

I requested of the medium's "control" that the most prominent person connected with the studio be allowed to speak to us. But Albert, the control, assured me that the woman, whom he called Elizabeth, was connected with that man. "He will come only if he is of a mind to. He entered the room a while ago."

I asked Albert to describe this man.

"Sharp features, from what I can see. You are closer to him. Clothes ... nineties, early 1900's."

After a while, the medium's lips started to move, and a gruff man's voice was heard: "*Get out* ... get out of my house."

Somewhat taken aback by this greeting, I started to explain to our visitor that we were his friends and here to help him. But he didn't mellow.

"I don't know who you are . . . who is everybody here. Don't have friends."

"I am here to help you," I said, and tried to calm the ghost's suspicions. But our visitor was not impressed.

"I want help, but not from you . . . *I'll find it!*"

He wouldn't tell us what he was looking for. There were additional requests for us to get out of his house. Finally, the ghost pointed the medium's arm toward the stove and intoned—"I put it there!" A sudden thought inspired me, and I said, lightly—"We found it already."

Rage took hold of the ghost in an instant. "You took it . . . you betrayed me . . . it is mine . . . I was a good man."

I tried in vain to pry his full name from him.

He moaned. "I am sick all over now. Worry, worry, worry. Give it to me."

I promised to return "it," if he would cooperate with us.

In a milder tone he said, "I wanted to make it so pretty. *It won't move.*"

I remembered how concerned La Farge had been with his beautiful altar painting, and that it should not fall *again*. I wondered if he knew how much time had passed.

"Who is President of the United States now?" I asked.

Our friend was petulant. "I don't know. I am sick. William McKinley." But then he volunteered—"I knew him. Met him. In Boston. Last year. Many years ago. Who are you? I don't know any friends. *I am in my house.*"

"What is your full name?"

"Why is that so hard? I know William and I don't know my *own* name."

I have seen this happen before. A disturbed spirit sometimes cannot recall his own name or address.

"Do you know you have passed over?"

"I live here," he said, quietly now. "Times changed. I know I am not what I used to be. *It is there!*"

When I asked what he was looking for, he changed the subject to Bertha, without explaining who Bertha was.

But as he insisted on finding "it," I finally said, "You are welcome to get up and look for it."

"I am bound in this chair and can't move."

"Then tell us where to look for it."

After a moment's hesitation, he spoke. "On the chimney, in back . . . it was over there. I will find it, but I can't move now . . . *I made a mistake* . . . I can't talk like this."

And suddenly he was gone.

As it was getting on to half past ten, the medium was awakened. The conversation among the guests then turned to any feelings they might have had during the seance. Miss Archer was asked about the building.

"It was put up in 1856," she replied, "and is a copy of a similar studio building in Paris."

"Has there ever been any record of a murder committed in this studio?" I asked.

"Yes . . . between 1870 and 1900, *a young girl went through one of these windows.* But I did not mention this in my article, as it *apparently* was unconnected with the La Farge story."

"What about Elizabeth? And Margaret?"

"That was remarkable of the medium," Miss Archer

nodded. "You see, Elizabeth was La Farge's wife . . . and Margaret, well, she also fits in with his story."

For the first time, the name La Farge had been mentioned in the presence of the medium. But it meant nothing to her in her conscious state.

Unfortunately, the ghost could not be convinced that his search for the plans was unnecessary, for La Farge's genius as an architect and painter has long since belonged to time.

A few weeks after this seance, I talked to an advertising man named Douglas Baker. To my amazement, he, too, had at one time occupied Studio 22. Although aware of the stories surrounding the building, he had scoffed at the idea of a ghost. But one night he was roused from deep sleep by the noise of someone opening and closing drawers. Sitting up in bed, he saw a man in Victorian opera clothes in his room, which was dimly lit by the skylight and windows. Getting out of bed to fence off the intruder, he found himself alone, just as others had before him.

No longer a scoffer, he talked to others in the building, and was able to add one more episode to the La Farge case. It seems a lady was passing No. 51 one bleak afternoon when she noticed an odd-looking gentleman in opera clothes standing in front of the building. For no reason at all, the woman exclaimed, "My, you're a funny-looking man!"

The gentleman in the opera cloak looked at her in rage. "Madam—how dare you!"

And with that, *he went directly through the building—the wall of the building, that is!*

Passers-by revived the lady.

Now there is a modern apartment building at 51 West 10th Street. Is John La Farge still roaming its ugly modern corridors? Last night, I went into the Church of the Ascension, gazed at the marvelous altar painting, and prayed a little that he shouldn't *have to.*

THE HAUNTINGS
AT SEVEN OAKS

Eleanor Small is a charming woman in her late forties who dabbles in real estate and business. She comes from a very good family which once had considerable wealth, and is what is loosely termed "social" today. She wasn't the kind of person one would suspect of having any interest in the supernatural.

One evening, as we were discussing other matters, the conversation got around to ghosts. To my amazement, Eleanor was fascinated by the topic; so much so, that I could not help asking her if by chance she knew of a haunted house somewhere for me to investigate!

"Indeed I do," was the reply, and this is how I first heard about Seven Oaks. In Mamaroneck, New York, up in posh Westchester County, there stood until very recently a magnificent colonial mansion known as Seven Oaks. Situated near the edge of Long Island Sound, it was one of the show places of the East. Just as did so many fine old mansions, this one gave way to a "development," and now there are a number of small, insignificant, ugly modern houses dotting the grounds of the large estate.

During the Battle of Orient Point, one of the bloodier engagements of the Revolutionary War, the mansion was British-held, and American soldiers, especially the wounded, were often smuggled out to Long Island Sound via an "underground railway," passing through the mansion.

"When I was a young girl," Eleanor said, "I spent many years with my mother and my stepfather at Seven Oaks, which we then owned. I was always fascinated by the many secret passageways which honeycombed the house."

The entrance was from the library; some books would slide back, and a slender wooden staircase appeared. Gaslight jets had been installed in the nineteenth century to light these old passages. A colored butler working for Eleanor's parents stumbled onto them by chance.

"When did you first hear about ghosts?" I asked.

"We moved into the house about June 1932. Right away, a neighbor by the name of Mabel Merker told us that the place was *haunted. Of course,* we paid no attention to her."

"Of course." I nodded wryly.

"But it wasn't too long before Mother changed her mind about that."

"You mean she saw the ghost?"

Eleanor nodded. "Regularly, *practically every night.*" Eleanor's mother had described her as a woman of about forty-five, with long blond hair and a sweet expression on her face. One of these apparitions had its comic aspects, too.

"Mother had her private bathroom, which connected directly with her bedroom. One night, after all doors had been locked and Mother knew there was no one about any more, she retired for the night. Entering the bathroom from her bedroom, she left the connecting door open in the knowledge that her privacy could not possibly be disturbed! Suddenly, looking up, *she saw, back in her room, the ghost standing and beckoning to her in the bathroom,* as if she wanted to tell her something of utmost urgency. There was such an expression of sadness and frustration on the wraith's face, Mother could never forget it."

"But what did she *do?*" I asked.

"She approached the apparition, but when she got halfway across the room, the ghost just evaporated into thin air."

"And this was in good light, and the apparition was not shadowy or vaporous?"

"Oh no, it looked just like someone of flesh and blood—until that last moment when she *dissolved before Mother's eyes.*"

"Was your mother very upset?"

"Only at first. Later she got used to the idea of having a ghost around. Once she saw her up on the second floor, in the master bedroom. There she was standing in front of the two beds. Mother wondered what she could do to help her, but the ghost again vanished."

"Did she ever hear her talk or make any kind of noise?" I asked.

"Not talk, but noise—well, at the time Mother moved into the house, the previous owner, Mrs. Warren, still maintained a few things of her own in a closet in the house, and she was in the habit of returning there occasionally to pick some of them up, a few at a time. One evening Mother heard some footsteps, but thought them to be Mrs. Warren's.

"The next day, however, she found out that no one had been to the house. Our family dog frequently barked loudly and strongly before the fireplace, at *something* or *someone* we could not see, but evidently he *could*."

"Did anyone else see the ghost?"

"The servants, especially the colored men, constantly complained of *being pulled from their beds,* in the servants' quarters, by unseen hands. It was as if someone wanted their attention, but there never was anyone there when the lights were turned on."

"She probably wanted to talk to someone, as ghosts often do!" I said. Communication and inability to be heard or seen by the people of flesh and blood is the main agony of a wraith.

"That must be so," Eleanor nodded, "because there was another incident some years later that seems to confirm it. My stepfather's son and his seventeen-year-old bride came to live at Seven Oaks. The girl was part Indian, and extremely sensitive. They were given a room on the top floor of the old mansion, with a double bed in the center.

"One night they retired early, and the son was already in bed, while his wife stood nearby in the room. Suddenly, as she looked on with horror, she saw her *husband bodily pulled out of bed by unseen hands.* His struggle was in vain.

"The next morning, the young couple left Seven Oaks, never to return."

THE CENTRAL
PARK WEST GHOST

Mrs. M. Daly Hopkins was a lady of impeccable taste, and gracious surroundings meant a great deal to her and her husband. Consequently, when they decided to look for a new apartment, they directed their steps toward Central Park West, which in the thirties had become one of New York's more desirable residential areas.

As they were walking up the tree-lined street, they noticed a man in working overalls hanging up a sign on a building, reading "Apartment for Rent." The man turned out to be the superintendent of one of three identical gray five-story buildings on the corner of 107th Street and Central Park West.

Mrs. Hopkins, who reported her uncanny experiences

in a story entitled "Ten Years with a Ghost,"* was over-joyed. The location was perfect; now if only the apartment suited them! With hearts beating a trifle faster, the Hop-kinses approached the building.

The apartment for rent was on the top floor, that is, it occupied the southeast corner of the fifth floor of the build-ing, and it contained a total of eight rooms. This seemed ideal to the Hopkinses, who needed plenty of space for themselves, their small son, and his nurse.

It seemed the former tenants had just moved out, after living in the apartment for many years. Most of the people in the building, the superintendent added, had been there a long time. The tenants of this particular apartment had been just husband and wife. By November of the same year, the Hopkins family was settled in the new apartment.

Nothing unusual happened during the first few weeks of their stay, except that on a number of occasions Mrs. Hopkins heard her housekeeper cry out, as if surprised by someone or something!

Finally, the middle-aged woman came to Mrs. Hopkins, and said: "Something's strange about this place. I often feel someone standing behind me, and yet, when I turn around, there is nobody there!"

Mrs. Hopkins, naturally, tried to talk her out of her apprehensions, but to no avail. For two years Annie, the housekeeper, tolerated the "unseen visitor." Then she quit. She just could not go on like this, she explained. "*Somebody*

---

* *Fate,* July, 1954.

keeps turning my doorknob. I am not a superstitious person, but I do believe you have a *ghost* here."

Mrs. Hopkins wondered why no one else in the apartment noticed anything unusual. After Annie left, Josephine, a colored woman, was hired, and slept in the apartment. Before long, Josephine, too, kept exclaiming in surprise, just as Annie had done for so long.

Finally, Josephine came to see Mrs. Hopkins and asked if she could talk to her. Mrs. Hopkins sat back to listen.

"This apartment is haunted," Josephine said.

Mrs. Hopkins was not surprised. She admitted openly now that there was an "unseen guest" at the apartment, but she loved the apartment too much to give it up. "We'll just have to live with that ghost!" she replied. Josephine laughed, and said it was all right with her, too.

She felt the ghost was female, and from that day on, for seven and a half years, Josephine would speak aloud to the ghost on many occasions, addressing her always as "Miss Flossie" and asking the unquiet spirit to tell her what was troubling her so much. Finally, one morning, Josephine came into Mrs. Hopkins' room and told her that she knew why "Miss Flossie" could not find rest.

"Miss Flossie killed herself, Ma'am," she said quietly.

Josephine never actually *saw* the ghost, for "no matter how quick I turn, the ghost is even quicker" to disappear. But as is the case so often with children, the Hopkinses' small son *did see* her. The boy was then just four years old.

He had been asleep for several hours that particular night, when Mrs. Hopkins heard him call out for her. Since the "nanna" was out for the evening, Mrs. Hopkins rushed to his side. The boy said a "lady visitor waked me up when she kissed me." Mrs. Hopkins insisted that she and her husband were the only ones at home. The boy insisted that he had seen this woman, and that she looked like "one of those dolls little girls play with."

Mrs. Hopkins calmed her boy, and after he had returned to sleep, she went to her husband and brought him up to date on this entire ghost business. He didn't like it at all. But somehow the household settled down to routine again, and it was several years before another manifestation occurred, or was noticed, at least.

One night, while her son was in boarding school and her husband out of town on business, Mrs. Hopkins found herself all alone in the apartment. The "nanna" had returned to England. It was a quiet, rainy night, and Mrs. Hopkins did not feel unduly nervous, especially as "Miss Flossie" had not been active for so long.

Sometime after going to bed, Mrs. Hopkins was awakened by someone calling her name. "Mrs. Hop-kins! Mrs. Hop-kins!" There was a sense of urgency about the voice, which seemed to be no different from that of someone close by. Mrs. Hopkins responded immediately. "Yes, what is it?" Fully awake now, she noticed by her clock that the time was 1:00 A.M. Suddenly she became aware of an entirely different sound. Overhead, on the roof, there were footsteps, and somehow she knew it was a burglar. Jumping from bed, Mrs. Hopkins examined the hall door. The three locks were all off. She tried to telephone the superintendent, but found the line had been cut! Without a moment's hesitation, she retraced her steps to the bedroom, and *locked herself in the room.*

The next morning, the superintendent informed Mrs. Hopkins that the two other houses in the block had their top floor apartments burglarized during the night, but her apartment had somehow been spared! Mrs. Hopkins smiled wanly. How could she explain that a ghost had saved her that night?

One evening Mrs. Hopkins and her husband returned from the theater and found a small black kitten crying on the front doorstep of the house. She felt pity for the kitten, and took it into the apartment, locking it into the maid's room for the night. At first they thought it was a neighbor's cat, but nobody came to claim it, and in the end they kept it.

The cat behaved strangely right from the start. Dashing through the apartment with fur disarranged, she seemed terrified of something. Josephine assured Mrs. Hopkins that the ghost hated the kitten, and would kill it before long.

A week later, Mrs. Hopkins sat alone in a comfortable chair, reading. It was evening, and the kitten was curled up, sleeping peacefully nearby. Suddenly the cat looked toward the doorway leading into the hall. Getting up, she seemed to see someone enter the room, pass in front of Mrs. Hopkins, and finally stand directly behind her. The cat seemed terrified. Finally, Mrs. Hopkins said, "Kitty, don't be afraid of Miss Flossie." The cat relaxed, but not Mrs. Hopkins, who felt a terrific chill.

When her husband returned, she insisted they give up the apartment. The ghost had become too much for her. No sooner said than done, and two weeks later, they were living at the other end of town.

One night at dinner Mr. Hopkins mentioned that he had just learned more about their former apartment from one of the old tenants he had accidentally met. At the time when they rented the place, the superintendent told them the previous tenants had moved out "ten minutes before." What he had neglected to tell them, however, was *how*. The Hopkinses had come there *ten minutes after the funeral*. The wife of the former tenant had committed suicide in the living room. Mrs. Hopkins' curiosity was aroused. She went to see a Mrs. Foran, who lived at the old place directly below where their apartment had been.

"What sort of woman was this lady who died here?" she asked her.

Well, it seemed that the couple had been living elsewhere before their marriage without benefit of clergy. After they got married, they moved to this place, to make a fresh start.

But the wife was still unhappy. During the three years of their tenancy, she *imagined* the neighbors were gossiping about her. Actually, the neighbors knew nothing of their past, and cared less. "But," Mrs. Foran added as an afterthought, "she didn't *belong* here."

"Why not?" wondered Mrs. Hopkins.

"Because she had bleached hair, that's why!" replied Mrs. Foran.

Mrs. Hopkins couldn't help smiling, because she realized how right Josephine had been in calling *the spook* "Miss Flossie."

In July 1960, I decided to pay "Miss Flossie" a visit. I first located Mrs. Hopkins in Newmarket, Canada. My request for information was answered by Mrs. Hopkins' sister, Helena Daly.

"Since my sister is very handicapped following a stroke," she wrote, "I shall be pleased to give you the information you wish, as I lived there with them for a short time, but did not meet the ghost.

"The location is at 471 Central Park West, northwest corner of 106th Street, a top-floor apartment with windows facing south and also east, overlooking Central Park.

"Wishing you every success, yours truly, Helen M. Daly."

I located the house all right, even though it was at 107th Street. The apartment on the top floor was locked. I located a ground-floor tenant who knew the name of the family now living in it. The name was Hernandez, but that didn't get me into the apartment by a long shot. Three letters remained unanswered. The rent collector gave me the name of the superintendent. He didn't have a key either. The entire neighborhood had changed greatly in character since the Hopkinses lived there. The whole area, and of course the building at 471 Central Park West, was now populated by Spanish-speaking Puerto Ricans.

Weeks went by. All my efforts to contact the Hernandez family proved fruitless. There was no telephone, and they never seemed to be home when I called. Finally, I decided to send a letter announcing my forthcoming visit three days hence at one thirty in the afternoon, and would they please be in, as I had the permission of their landlord to see them.

I was determined to hold a seance *outside* their very door-step, if necessary, hoping that my Sensitive, Mrs. Meyers, would somehow catch at least part of the vibratory element, and atmosphere, of the place. I also invited a Mr. Lawrence, a newspaper writer, to come along as a witness.

To my surprise, the seance on the doorstep was unneces-sary. When the three of us arrived at the apartment, some-what out of breath after climbing four flights of stairs on a hot summer day, the door was immediately opened by a nicely-dressed young man who introduced himself as Mr. Hernandez, owner of the flat. He led us through the large apartment into the living room at the corner of the building, the very room I was most interested in.

Mr. Hernandez spoke excellent English. He explained that he was a furniture repairman employed by one of the large hotels, and that he and his family—we saw a young wife and child—lived in the apartment. They had never seen nor heard anything unusual. He did not believe in "vibrations" or the supernatural, but had no objection to our sitting down and gathering what impressions we could. I had maintained in my letters all along that "a famous lit-erary figure" had once occupied his apartment and we wanted to visit the rooms for that reason, as I was doing an article on this person. It doesn't pay to tell the person whose apartment you want to visit that it's his ghost you're after.

Mrs. Meyers sat down on the comfortable couch near the window, and the rest of us took seats around her. Her first impressions of the room came through immediately.

"I hear a woman's voice calling Jamie or Janie. . . . There is an older woman, kind of emaciated looking, with gray hair, long nose, wide eyes, bushy eyebrows. Then there is a black cat. Something is upsetting Jamie. There's a squeaking rocking chair, a man with a booming voice, reciting lines, heavy-set, he wears a cutaway coat . . . man is heavy in the middle, has a mustache, standup collar with wings, dark tie . . . there's something wrong with his finger . . . a wedding band? A remark *about a wedding band*?"

Mrs. Meyers looked around the carefully furnished, spotlessly clean room, and continued. "A small boy, about twelve. Someone here used to live *with the dead* for a very long time, treated as if they were alive. Just stay here, never go out, if I go out, *he* is not going to come back again, so I'll remain here! I look from the window and see him coming out of the carriage. We have dinner every night." Suddenly, Mrs. Meyers started to inhale rapidly, and an expression of fear crept upon her face.

"Gas—always have one burner—gas! Somebody is still disturbed about Jamie. I get the letters M. B. or B. M. I feel lots of people around. There is a to-do in court. Now someone walks around the outside that can't be seen. Wants to come in by the window.

"It's like a nightmare, very dark, can't look out the window. I am a mess, and I'm going to fall if I let go. There's a body laid in a casket in this room, but very few flowers; the name on the silver plaque reads Stevens or Stevenson; the curtains are drawn, it's very dark, there are candles and a body in the casket."

I asked Mrs. Meyers if she felt any restless spirits about the place still.

"The restlessness is dimming," she replied. "It was there in the past, but is much dimmer now, because a religious person lives here."

Did she get any other impressions?

"The police had something to do here, they wear long coats, the coffin contains a person in black."

After we had left the apartment, I compared Mrs. Meyer's impressions to the material in the 1954 story, which I had never shown or mentioned to her. There was a small son, and the description of the "older woman" fitted Mrs. Hopkins, as did the black cat. Mrs. Meyers' statement, that "something was wrong with his finger . . . a wedding band!" recalled the fact that the couple had been living together as man and wife for years without being married, and had this fact not disturbed the ghost so much?

The gas explosion and the funeral following "Miss Flossie's" suicide were factual. M. is Mrs. Hopkins initial and "M. B." may have been "M. D.," which is M. Daly, Mrs. Hopkins' maiden name. "Someone walking on the outside" refers to the burglar episode. Police and the coffin make sense where suicide is involved.

Shortly after our seance, I received word that Mrs. Hopkins had passed on. Now perhaps she and "Miss Flossie" can become better acquainted.

THE GHOSTS
AT ST. MARK'S

Despite the fact that most religious faiths, and their clergy, take a dim view of ghosts and hauntings, there are many recorded cases of supernormal goings-on in churches and cemeteries. One such place of worship is New York's famed old *St. Mark's-in-the-Bouwerie church*, located at the corner of Second Avenue and 10th Street.

Originally the site of a chapel erected in 1660 by Peter Stuyvesant for the Dutch settlers of New Amsterdam, it became the governor's burial ground in 1672. The Stuyvesant vault was permanently sealed in 1953, when the last member of the family died. A century after the death of the governor, the family had adopted the Episcopalian faith, and a grandson, also named Peter Stuyvesant, gave the land and some cash to build on the same spot the present church of

St. Mark's. It was completed in 1799 and has been in service continuously since. No major repairs, additions, or changes were made in the building.

The surrounding neighborhood is now one of the worst in New York, although it was once a highly respected one. But even in the confines of the Bowery, there is a legend that St. Mark's is a haunted church. If nothing else, it effectively keeps the neighborhood's colorful alcoholics at a distance!

I talked to the Reverend Richard E. McEvoy, now Archdeacon of St. John's, but for many years rector of St. Mark's, about any apparitions he or others might have seen in the church. Legend, of course, has old Peter Stuyvesant rambling about now and then. The Reverend proved to be a keen observer, and quite neutral in the matter of ghosts. He himself had not seen anything unusual. But there was a man, a churchgoer, whom he had known for many years. This man always sat in a certain pew on the right side of the church.

Queried by the rector about his peculiar insistence on that seat, the man freely admitted it was because from there he could see "her"—the "her" being a female wraith who appeared in the church to listen to the sermon, and then disappeared again. At the spot he had chosen, he could always be next to her! I pressed the rector about any *personal* experiences. Finally he thought that he had seen something like a figure in white out of the corner of one eye, a figure that passed, and quickly disappeared. That was ten years ago.

On the rector's recommendation, I talked to Foreman

Cole, the man who comes to wind the clock at regular intervals, and who has been in and around St. Mark's for the past twenty-six years.

Mr. Cole proved to be a ready talker. Some years ago, Cole asked his friend Ray Bore, organist at a Roman Catholic church nearby, to have a look at the church organ. The church was quite empty at the time, which was 1:00 A.M. Nevertheless, Cole saw "someone" in the balcony.

About fifteen years ago, Cole had another unusual experience. It was winter, and the church was closed to the public, for it was after 5:00 P.M. That evening it got dark early, but there was still some light left when Cole let himself into the building. Nobody was supposed to be in the church at that time, as Cole well knew, being familiar with the rector's hours.

Nevertheless, to his amazement, *he clearly saw a woman standing in the back of the church,* near the entrance door, in the center aisle. Thinking that she was a late churchgoer who had been locked in by mistake, and worried that she might stumble in the semidarkness, he called out to her, "Wait, lady, don't move till I turn the lights on."

He took his eyes off her for a moment and quickly switched the lights on. But he found himself alone; she had vanished into thin air from her spot well within the nave of the church.

Unnerved, Cole ran to the entrance door and found it firmly locked. He then examined all the windows and found them equally well secured.

I asked Cole if there was anything peculiar about the

woman's appearance. He thought for a moment, then said, "Yes, there was. She seemed to ignore me, looked right through me, and did not respond to my words."

Six weeks later, he had another supernormal experience. Again alone in the church, with all doors locked, he saw a man who looked to him like one of the Bowery derelicts outside. He wore shabby clothes, and did not seem to "belong" here. Quickly, Cole switched on the lights to examine his visitor. But he had vanished, exactly as the woman had before.

Cole has not seen any apparitions since, but some pretty strange noises have reached his ears. For one thing, there is frequent "banging" about the church, and "uncanny" feelings and chills in certain areas of the old church. On one occasion, Cole clearly heard someone coming up the stairs leading to the choir loft. Thinking it was the sexton, he decided to give him a scare, and hid to await the man at the end of the staircase. Only, nobody came. The steps were those of an *unseen man*!

Cole has no idea who the ghosts could be. He still takes care of the clock, and is reluctant to discuss his experiences with ordinary people, lest they think him mad. A man of forty-one, and quite healthy and realistic, Cole is sure of his memories.

Several days later, I asked Mary R. M., a singer and gifted psychic, to accompany me to the church and see if she could get any "impressions." It turned out that my friend had been to the church once before, last November, when she was rehearsing nearby. At that time, she was *sure* the place was haunted. We sat in one of the right-hand pews, and waited. We were quite alone in the church; the time was three in the afternoon, and it was quite still. Within a minute or so, Mary told me she felt "a man with a cane walking down the middle aisle behind us." Peter Stuyvesant, buried here, walked with a cane.

Then my friend pointed to the rear, and advised me that she "saw" a woman in wide skirts standing near the rear door of the church. She added: "I see a white shape floating away from that marble slab in the rear!"

So if you ever see someone dissolve into thin air at St. Mark's—don't be alarmed. It's only a ghost!

A VISIT WITH ALEXANDER HAMILTON'S GHOST

There stands at Number 27, Jane Street, in New York's picturesque artists' quarters, Greenwich Village, a mostly wooden house dating back to pre-Revolutionary days. In this house Alexander Hamilton was treated in his final moments. Actually, he died a few houses away, at 80 Jane Street, but No. 27 was the home of John Francis, his doctor, who attended him after the fatal duel with Aaron Burr.

However, the Hamilton house no longer exists, and the wreckers are now after the one of his doctor, now occupied by a writer and artist, Jean Karsavina, who has lived there since 1939.

The facts of Hamilton's untimely passing are well known; D. S. Alexander (in his *Political History of the State of New York*) reports that, because of political enmity, "Burr seems to have deliberately determined to kill him." A letter written by Hamilton calling Burr "despicable" and "not to be trusted with the reins of government" found its way into the press, and Burr demanded an explanation. Hamilton declined, and on June 11, 1804, at Weehawken, New Jersey, Burr took careful aim, and his first shot mortally wounded Hamilton. In the boat back to the city, Hamilton regained consciousness, but knew his end was near. He was taken to Dr. Francis' house and treated, but died within a few days at his own home, across the street.

Ever since moving into 27 Jane Street, Miss Karsavina has been aware of footsteps, creaking stairs, and the opening and closing of doors; and even the unexplained flushing of a toilet. On one occasion, she found the toilet chain still swinging, when there was no one around! "I suppose a toilet that flushes *would* be a novelty to someone from the eighteenth century," she is quoted in a brief newspaper account in June of 1957.*

She also has seen a blurred "shape," without being able to give details of the apparition; her upstairs tenant, however, reports that one night not so long ago, "a man in eighteenth-century clothes, with his hair in a queue" walked into her room, looked at her and walked out again.

Miss Karsavina turned out to be a well-read and charming lady who had accepted the possibility of living with a ghost under the same roof. Mrs. Meyers and I went to see

---

* *Fate,* June, 1957.

her in March 1960. The medium had no idea where we were going.

At first, Mrs. Meyers, still in waking condition, noticed a "shadow" of a man, old, with a broad face and bulbous nose; a woman with a black shawl whose name she thought was Deborah, and she thought "someone had a case"; she then described an altar of white lilies, a bridal couple, and a small coffin covered with flowers; then a very old woman in a coffin that was richly adorned, with relatives including a young boy and girl looking into the open coffin. She got the name of Mrs. Patterson, and the girl's as Miss Lucy. In another "impression" of the same premises, Mrs. Meyers described "an empty coffin, people weeping, talking, milling around, *and the American Flag atop the coffin*; in the coffin a man's hat, shoes with silver buckles, gold epaulettes. . . ." She then got close to the man and thought his lungs were filling with liquid and he died with a pain in his side.

Lapsing into semitrance at this point, Mrs. Meyers described a party of men in a small boat on the water, then a man wearing white pants and a blue coat with blood spilled over the pants. "Two boats were involved, and it is dusk," she added.

Switching apparently to another period, Mrs. Meyers felt that "something is going on in the cellar, they try to keep attention from what happens downstairs; there is a woman here, being stopped by two men in uniforms with short jackets and round hats with wide brims, and pistols. There is the sound of shrieking, the woman is pushed back violently, men are marching, someone who had been harbored here has to be given up, an old man in a nightshirt and red socks is being dragged out of the house into the snow."

In still another impression, Mrs. Meyers felt herself drawn up toward the rear of the house where "someone died in childbirth"; in fact, this type of death occurred "several times" in this house. Police were involved, too, but this event or chain of events is of a later period than the initial impressions, she felt. The name Henry Oliver or Oliver Henry came to her mind.

After her return to full consciousness, Mrs. Meyers remarked that there was a chilly area near the center of the downstairs room. There is; I feel it too. Mrs. Meyers "sees" the figure of a slender man, well-formed, over average height, in white trousers, black boots, dark blue coat and tails, white lace in front; *he is associated with George Washington and Lafayette,* and their faces appear to her, too; she feels Washington may have been in this house. The man she "sees" is a *general,* she can see his epaulettes. The old woman and the children seen earlier are somehow connected with this, too. He died young, and there "was fighting in a boat." Now Mrs. Meyers gets the name "W. Lawrence." She has a warm feeling about the owner of the house; he took in numbers of people, like refugees.

A "General Mills" stored supplies here—shoes, coats, almost like a military post; food is being handed out. The name Bradley is given. Then Mrs. Meyers sees an old man playing a cornet; two men in white trousers are "seen" seated at a long table, bent over papers, with a crystal chandelier above.

After the seance, Miss Karsavina confirmed that the house belonged to Hamilton's physician, and as late as 1825 was owned by a doctor, who happened to be the doctor for the Metropolitan Opera House. The cornet player might have been one of his patients.

In pre-Revolutionary days, the house may have been used as headquarters of an "underground railroad," around 1730, when the police tried to pick up the alleged instigators of the so-called "Slave Plot," evidently being sheltered here.

"Lawrence" may refer to the portrait of Washington by Lawrence which *used* to hang over the fireplace in the house. On the other hand, I found a T. Lawrence, M.D., at 146 Greenwich Street, *Elliot's Improved Double Directory for New-York* (1812); and a "Widow Patterson" is listed by Longworth (1803) at 177 William Street; a William Lawrence, druggist, at 80 John Street. According to Charles Burr Todd's *Story of the City of New York,* two of Hamilton's pallbearers were *Oliver* Wolcott and John L. *Lawrence.* The other names mentioned could not be found. The description of the man in white trousers is of course the perfect image of Hamilton, and the goings-on at the house with its many coffins, and women dying in childbirth, are indeed understandable for a doctor's residence.

It does not seem surprising that Alexander Hamilton's shade should wish to roam about the house of the man who tried, vainly, to save his life.

THE CONFERENCE
HOUSE GHOST

Only an hour or so by ferry boat from bustling Manhattan lies the remote charm of Staten Island, where many old houses and even farms still exist in their original form within the boundaries of New York City.

One of these old houses, and a major sight-seeing attraction, is the so-called "Conference House," where the British Commander, Lord Howe, received the American Conference delegation consisting of Benjamin Franklin, John Adams, and Edward Rutledge, on September 11, 1776. The purpose of the meeting was to convince the Americans that a peaceful solution should be found for the difficulties between England and the Colonies. The meeting proved unsuccessful, of course, and the Revolutionary War ensued.

The house itself is a sturdy white two-story building,

erected along typical English manor-house lines, in 1688, on a site known then as Bentley Manor in what is today Tottenville. There are two large rooms on the ground floor, and a staircase leading to an upper story, also divided into two rooms; a basement contains the kitchen and a vaultlike enclosure. The original owner of the house was Captain Billopp of the British Navy, and his descendants lived in the house until the close of the Revolutionary period.

Local legends have had the house "haunted" for many years. The story was that Billopp, a hard man, jilted his fiancee, and that she died of a broken heart in this very house. For several generations back, reports of noises, murmurs, sighs, moans, and pleas have been received and the old Staten Island *Transcript,* a local newspaper, has mentioned these strange goings-on over the years. When the house was being rebuilt, after having been taken over as a museum by the City, the workmen are said to have heard the strange noises, too.

It was against this background that I decided to investigate the house in the company of Mrs. Meyers, who was to be our Sensitive, and two friends, Rose de Simone and Pearl Winder, who were to be the "sitters," or assistants to the medium.

After we had reached Staten Island, and were about half an hour's drive from the house, Mrs. Meyers volunteered her impressions of the house which she was yet to see! She spoke of it as being white, the ground floor divided into two rooms, a brown table and eight chairs in the east room; the room on the west side of the house is the larger one, and lighter colored than the other room, and some silverware was on display in the room to the left.

Upon arriving at the house, I checked these statements; they were correct, except that the number of chairs was now only seven, not eight, and the silver display had been removed from its spot eight years before!

Mrs. Meyers' very first impression was the name "Butler"; later I found that the estate next door belonged to the Butler family, unknown, of course, to the medium.

We ascended the stairs; Mrs. Meyers sat down on the floor of the second-story room to the left. She described a woman named Jane, stout, white-haired, wearing a dark green dress and a fringed shawl, then mentioned the name *Howe*. It must be understood that the connection of Lord Howe with the house was totally unknown to all of us until *after* checking up on the history of the Conference House, later on.

Next Mrs. Meyers described a man with white hair, or a wig, wearing a dark coat with embroidery at the neck, tan breeches, dark shoes, and possessed of a wide, square face, a thick nose, and looking "Dutch." "The man died in this room," she added.

She then spoke of the presence of a small boy, about six, dressed in pantaloons and with his hair in bangs. The child born in this room was specially honored later, Mrs. Meyers felt. This might apply to Christopher Billopp, born at the house in 1737, who later became Richmond County representative in the Colonial Assembly. Also, Mrs. Meyers felt the "presence" of a big man in a fur hat, rather fat, wearing a skin coat and high boots, brass-buckle belt and black trousers; around him she felt boats, nets, sailing boats, and she heard a foreign, broad accent, also saw him in a four-masted ship of the square-rigger type. The initial T was given. Later, I learned that the Billopp family were prominent Tory leaders up to and during the Revolution.

This man, Mrs. Meyers felt, had a loud voice, broad forehead, high cheekbones, was a vigorous man, tall, with shaggy hair, and possibly Dutch. His name was Van B., she thought. She did not know that Billopp (or Van Billopp) was the builder of the house.

"I feel as if I'm being dragged somewhere by Indians," Mrs. Meyers suddenly said. "There is violence, somebody dies on a pyre of wood, two men, one white, one Indian; and on two sticks nearby are their scalps."

Later, I ascertained that Indian attacks were frequent here during the seventeenth and eighteenth centuries and that, in fact, a tunnel once existed as an escape route to the nearby waterfront, in case of hostile Indian sieges. Large numbers of arrowheads have been unearthed around the house.

Down in the cellar, Mrs. Meyers felt sure six people had been buried near the front wall during the Revolutionary War, all British soldiers; she thought eight more were buried elsewhere on the grounds and sensed the basement full of wounded "like a hospital." On investigation, I found that some members of Billopp's family were indeed buried on the grounds near the road; as for the British soldiers, there were frequent skirmishes around the house between Americans infiltrating from the nearby New Jersey shore, and the British, who held Staten Island since July 4, 1776. At one time, Captain Billopp, a British subject, was kidnapped by armed bands in his own house, and taken to New Jersey a prisoner of the Americans!

We returned to the upper part of the house once more. Suddenly, Mrs. Meyers felt impelled to turn her attention to the winding staircase. I followed with mounting excitement.

Descending the stairs, our medium suddenly halted her steps and pointed to a spot near the landing of the second story. "Someone was killed here with a crooked knife, a woman!" she said. There was horror on her face as if she were reliving the murder. On questioning the custodian, Mrs. Early, I discovered that Captain Billopp, in a rage, had indeed killed a female slave on that very spot!

THE
CLINTON COURT
GHOSTS

While casually leafing through the pages of *Tomorrow* magazine, a periodical devoted to psychical research in which my byline appears on occasion, I noticed a short piece by Wainwright Evans, called "Ghost in Crinoline." The article, written in the spring of 1959, told of a spectral inhabitant at number 422½ West 46th Street, in New York City. It seemed that Ruth Shaw, an artist who had for years lived in the rear section of the old building, which she had turned into a studio for herself, had spoken to Mr. Evans about her experiences. He had come to see her at Clinton Court, as the building still is called. There is a charming iron gate through which you pass by the main house into a court. Beyond the court rises an arcaded rear section, three stories high and possessed of an outdoor staircase leading to the top. This portion dates back to 1809, or perhaps even before, and was at one time used as the coach house of Governor DeWitt Clinton.

Miss Shaw informed Evans about the legends around the place, and in her painstaking manner told him of her conversations with ninety-year-old Mr. Oates, a neighborhood druggist. An English coachman, with a Danish wife, once lived in the rooms above the stables. The first ghost ever to be seen at Clinton Court was that of "Old Moor," a sailor hanged for mutiny at the Battery, and buried in Potter's Field, which was only a short block away from the house. Today, this cemetery has disappeared beneath the teeming tenement houses of the middle Westside, Hell's Kitchen's outer approaches. But "Old Moor," as it were, did not have far to go to haunt anyone. Clinton Court was the first big house in his path. The coachman's wife saw the apparition, and while running away from "Old Moor," fell down the stairs. This was the more unfortunate as she was expecting a child at the time. She died of the fall, but the child survived.

The irony of it was that soon the mother's ghost was seen around the Court, too, usually hanging around the baby. Thus, Ghost Number 2 joined the cast at the Governor's old house.

One of the grandchildren of the Clinton family, who had been told these stories, used to play "ghost" the way children nowadays play cops and robbers. This girl, named Margaret, used to put on old-fashioned clothes and run up and down the big stairs. One fine day, she tripped and fell down the stairs, making the game grim reality. Many have seen the pale little girl; Miss Shaw was among them. She described her as wearing a white blouse, full sleeves, and a crinoline. On one occasion, she saw the girl ghost skipping down the stairs *in plain daylight*—skipping is the right word, for a ghost need not actually "walk," but often floats just a little bit above ground, not quite touching it.

I thought it would be a good idea to give Miss Shaw a ring, but discovered there was no telephone at the address. Miss Shaw had moved away and even the local police sergeant could not tell me where the house was. The police assured me *there was no such number* as 422½ West 46th Street. Fortunately, I have a low opinion of police intelligence, so my search continued. Perhaps a dozen times I walked by numbers 424 and 420 West 46th Street before I discovered the strange archway at Number 420. I walked through it, somehow driven on by an inner feeling that I was on the right track. I was, for before me opened Clinton Court. It simply was tucked away in back of 420 and the new owners had neglected to put the 422½ number anywhere within sight. Now an expensive, remodeled apartment house, the original walls and arrangements were still intact.

On the wall facing the court, Number 420 proudly displayed a bronze plaque inscribed "Clinton Court—ca. 1840—Restored by the American Society for Preservation of Future Antiquities"! The rear building, where Miss Shaw's studio used to be, was now empty. Apparently the carpenters had just finished fixing the floors and the apartment was up for rent. I thought that fortunate, for it meant we could get into the place without worrying about a tenant. But there was still the matter of finding out who the landlord was, and getting permission. It took me several weeks and much conversation, until I finally got permission to enter the place one warm evening in August 1960.

Meanwhile I had been told by the superintendent that an old crony by the name of Mrs. Butram lived next door, at Number 424, and that she might know something of interest. I found Mrs. Butram without difficulty. Having been warned that she kept a large number of pets, my nose led me to her door. For twenty-five years, she assured me, she had lived here, and had heard many a story about the ghost next door. She had never seen anything herself, but when I pressed her for details, she finally said—

"Well, they say it's a young girl of about sixteen. . . . One of the horses they used to keep back there broke loose and frightened her. Ran down the stairs, and fell to her death. That's what they say!"

I thanked Mrs. Butram, and went home. I called my good friend Mrs. Meyers, and asked her to accompany me to a haunted house, without telling her any more than that.

To my surprise, Mrs. Meyers told me on the phone that she thought she could see the place clairvoyantly that very instant.

"There is a pair of stairs outside of a house, and a woman in white, in a kind of backyard."

This conversation took place on August 9, a week before

Mrs. Meyers knew anything about the location or nature of our "case."

About a week later, we arrived together at Clinton Court, and proceeded immediately into the ground-floor studio apartment of the former coach house. In subdued light, we sat quietly on the shabby, used-up furniture.

"Let me look around and see what I get," Mrs. Meyers said, and rose. Slowly I followed her around the apartment, which lay in ghostly silence. Across the yard, the windows of the front section were ablaze with light and the yard itself was lit up by floodlights. But it was a quiet night. The sounds of "Hell's Kitchen" did not intrude into our atmosphere, as if someone bent on granting us privacy for a little while were muffling them.

"I feel funny in the head, bloated . . . you understand I am *her* now . . . there are wooden steps from the right on the outside of the place—"

Mrs. Meyers pointed at the wall. "There, where the wall now is; they took them down, I'm sure." On close inspection, I noticed traces of something that may have been a staircase.

"A woman in white, young, teen-ager, she's a bride, she's fallen down those steps on her wedding night, her head is battered in—"

Horror came over Mrs. Meyers' face. Then she continued. "It is cold, the dress is so flimsy, flowing; she is disappointed, for someone has disappointed *her.*"

Deep in thought, Mrs. Meyers sat down in one of the

chairs in a little room off the big, sunken living room that formed the main section of the studio apartment now, as the new owners had linked two apartments to make one bigger one.

"She has dark hair, blue eyes, light complexion, I'd say she's in her middle teens and wears a pretty dress, almost like a nightgown, the kind they used to have seventy-five or a hundred years ago. But now I see her in a gingham or checkered dress with high neck, long sleeves, a white hat, she's ready for a trip, only someone doesn't come. There is crying, disappointment. Then there is a seafaring man also, with a blue hat with shiny visor, a blue coat. He's a heavy-set man."

I thought of "Old Moor." Mrs. Meyers was getting her impressions all at the same time. Of course, she knew nothing of either the young girl ghost nor the sailor.

Now the medium told a lively tale of a young girl ready to marry a young man, but pursued by another, older man. "I can hear her scream!" She grabbed her own throat, and violently suppressed a scream, the kind of sound that might have invited an unwelcome audience to our seance!

"Avoiding the man, she rushes up the stairs, it is a slippery and cold day around Christmas. She's carrying something heavy, maybe wood and coal, and it's the eve of her marriage, but she's pushed off the roof. There are two women, the older one had been berating the girl, and pushed her out against the fence, and over she went. It was cold and slippery and nobody's fault. But instead of a wedding, there is a funeral."

The medium was now in full trance. Again, a scream is suppressed, then the voice changes and another personality speaks through Mrs. Meyers.

"Who are you?" I said, as I always do on such occasions. Identification is a must when you communicate with ghosts.

Instead, the stranger said anxiously—"Mathew!"

"Who is Mathew?" I said.

"Why won't he come, where is he? Why?"

"Who are you?"

"Bernice."

"How old are you?"

"Seventeen."

"What year is this?"

"Eighty."

But then the anguish came to the fore again.

"Where is he, he has the ring . . . my head . . . Mathew, Mathew . . . she pushed me, she is in hell. I'm ready to go, I'm dressed, we're going to father. I'm dressed. . . ."

As she repeated her pleas, the voice gradually faded out. Then, just as suddenly as she had given way to the stranger, Mrs. Meyers' own personality returned.

As we walked out of the gloomy studio apartment, I mused about the story that had come from Mrs. Meyers' lips. Probably servant girls, I thought, and impossible to trace. Still, she got the young girl, her falling off the stairs, the stairs themselves, and the ghostly sailor. Clinton Court is still haunted all right!

I looked up at the reassuringly lighted modern apartments around the yard, and wondered if the ghosts knew the difference. If you ever happen to be in "Hell's Kitchen," step through the archway at 420 West 46th Street into the yard, and if you're real, real quiet, and a bit lucky, of course, perhaps you will meet the teen-age ghost in her white dress or crinoline—but beware of "Old Moor" and his language—you know what sailors are like!

THE
HOUSE GHOST
OF BERGENVILLE

About a year ago, Mrs. Ethel Meyers, who has frequently accompanied me on ghost-hunting expeditions, heard from friends living in Bergen County, New Jersey, about some unusual happenings at their very old house. They are busy people of considerable prominence in the theater, but eventually the "safari for ghost" was organized, and Mr. B., the master of the house, picked us up in his car and drove us to Bergen County. The house turned out to be a beautifully preserved pre-Revolutionary house set within an enclosure of tall trees and lawns.

The building had been started in 1704, I later learned, and the oldest portion was the right wing; the central portion was added in the latter part of the eighteenth century, and the final, frontal portion was built from old materials about fifty years ago, carefully preserving the original style of the house. The present owners had acquired it about a year ago from a family who had been in possession for several generations. The house was then empty, and the B.'s refurbished it completely in excellent taste with antiques of the period.

After they moved into the house, they slept for a few days on a mattress on the enclosed porch, which skirted the west wing of the house. Their furniture had not yet arrived, and they didn't mind roughing it for a short while. It was summer, and not too cool.

In the middle of the night, Mrs. B. suddenly awoke with the uncanny feeling that there was *someone else* in the house, besides her husband and herself. She got up and walked toward the corridor-like extension of the enclosed porch running along the back of the house. There she clearly distinguished the figure of a man, seemingly white, with a beard, wearing what she described as "something ruffly white." She had the odd sensation that this man belonged to a much earlier period than the present. The light was good enough to see the man clearly for about five minutes, in which she was torn between fear of the intruder and curiosity. Finally, she approached him, and saw him *literally dissolve before her very eyes*! At the same time, she had the odd sensation that the stranger came to look *them* over, wondering what they were doing in *his* house! Mrs. B., a celebrated actress and choreographer, is not a scoffer, nor is she easily susceptible. Ghosts to her are something one can discuss intelligently. Since her husband shared this view, they inquired of the former owner about any possible hauntings.

"I've never heard of any or seen any," Mr. S. told them, "but my daughter-in-law has never been able to sleep in the oldest part of the house. Said there was too much going on there. Also, one of the neighbors claims he saw *something*."

Mr. S. wasn't going to endanger his recent real-estate transaction with too many ghostly tales. The B.'s thanked him and settled down to life in their colonial house.

But they soon learned that theirs was a busy place indeed. Both are artistic and very intuitive, and they soon became aware of the presence of unseen forces.

One night Mrs. B. was alone at home, spending the evening in the upper story of the house. There was nobody downstairs. Suddenly she heard the downstairs front door open and shut. There was no mistaking the very characteristic and complex sound of the opening of this ancient lock! Next, she heard footsteps, and sighed with relief. Apparently her husband had returned much earlier than expected. Quickly, she rushed down the stairs to welcome him. There was nobody there. There was no one in front of the door. All she found was the cat in a strangely excited state!

Sometime after, Mr. B. came home. For his wife these were anxious hours of waiting. He calmed her as best he could, having reservations about the whole incident. Soon these doubts were to be dispelled completely.

This time Mrs. B. was away and Mr. B. was alone in the downstairs part of the house. The maid was asleep in her room, the B.'s child fast asleep upstairs. It was a peaceful evening, and Mr. B. decided to have a snack. He found himself in the kitchen, which is located at the western end of the downstairs part of the house, *when he suddenly heard a car drive up*. Next, there were the distinct sounds of the front door opening and closing again. As he rushed to the front door, he heard the dog bark furiously. But again, there was no one either inside or outside the house!

Mr. B., a star and director, and as rational a man as could be, wondered if he had imagined these things. But he knew he had not. What he had heard were clearly the noises of an arrival. While he was still trying to sort out the meaning of all this, another strange thing happened.

A few evenings later, he found himself alone in the downstairs living room, when he heard carriage wheels outside grind to a halt. He turned his head toward the door, wondering who it might be at this hour. The light was subdued, but good enough to read by. He didn't have to wait long. A short, husky man walked into the room *through* the closed door; then, without paying attention to Mr. B., turned and walked out into the oldest part of the house, again *through a closed door*!

"What did he look like to you?" I asked.

"He seemed dotted, as if he were made of thick, solid dots, and he wore a long coat, the kind they used to wear around 1800. He probably was the same man my wife encountered."

"You think he is connected with the oldest part of the house?"

"Yes, I think so. About a year ago I played some very old

lute music, the kind popular in the eighteenth century, in there—and something happened to the atmosphere in the room. As if someone were listening quietly and peacefully."

But it wasn't always as peaceful in there. A day before our arrival, Mrs. B. had lain down, trying to relax. But she could not stay in the old room. "There was someone there," she said simply.

The B.'s weren't the only ones to hear and see ghosts. Last summer, two friends of the B.'s were visiting them, and everybody was seated in the living room, when in plain view of all, the screen door to the porch opened and closed again *by its own volition*! Needless to add, the friends didn't stay long.

Only a day before our visit, another friend had tried to use the small washroom in the oldest part of the house. Suddenly, he felt chills coming on and rushed out of the room, telling Mrs. B. that "someone was looking at him."

At this point, dinner was ready, and a most delicious repast it was. Afterwards we accompanied the B.'s into the oldest part of their house, a low-ceilinged room dating back to the year 1704. Two candles provided the only light. Mrs. Meyers got into a comfortable chair, and gradually drifted into trance.

"Marie . . . Catherine . . . who calls?" she mumbled.

"Who is it?" I inquired.

"Pop . . . live peacefully . . . love. . . ."

"What is your name?" I wanted to know.

"Achabrunn. . . ."

I didn't realize it at the time, but a German family named Achenbach had built the house and owned it for several generations. Much later still, I found out that one of the children of the builder had been called Marian.

I continued my interrogation.

"Who rules this country?"

"The Anglish. George."

"What year is this?"

"56. 1756."

"When did you stay here?"

"Always. Pop. My house. *You* stay with *me*."

Then the ghost spoke haltingly of his family, his children, of which he had nine, three of whom had gone away.

"What can we do for you?" I said, hoping to find the reason for the many disturbances.

"Yonder over side hill, hillock, three buried . . . flowers there."

"Do you mean," I said, "that we should put flowers on these graves?"

The medium seemed excited.

"*Ach Gott, ja, machs gut.*" With this the medium crossed herself.

"What is your name?" I asked again.

"Oterich . . . Oblich. . . ." The medium seemed hesitant as if the ghost were searching his memory for his own name. Later, I found that the name given was pretty close to that of another family having a homestead next door.

The ghost continued.

"She lady . . . I not good. I very stout heart, I look up to good-blood lady, I make her good . . . Kathrish, holy lady, I worship lady . . . they rest on hill too, with three. . . ."

After the seance, I found a book entitled *Pre-Revolutionary Dutch Houses and Families in Northern New Jersey and Southern New York*. It was here that I discovered the tradition that a poor shepherd from Saxony married a woman above his station, and built this very house. The year 1756 was correct.

But back to my interrogation. "Why don't you rest on the hillock?"

"I take care of . . . four . . . hillock . . . Petrish. Ladian, Annia, Kathrish. . . ."

Then, as if taking cognizance of us, he added—"To care for you, that's all I want."

Mrs. B. nodded and said softly, "You're always welcome here."

Afterward, I found that there were indeed some graves on the hill beyond the house. The medium now pointed toward the rear of the house, and said, "Gate . . . we put intruders there, he won't get up any more. Gray Fox made trouble, Indian man, I keep him right there."

"Are there any passages?"

"Yeah. Go dig through. When Indian come, they no find."

"Where?"

"North hillock, still stone floor there, ends here."

From Mr. B. I learned that underground passages are known to exist between this house and the so-called "Slave House," across the road.

The ghost then revealed that his wife's father, an Englishman, had built the passage, and that stores were kept in it along with Indian bones.

"Where were you born?" I inquired.

"Here. Bergenville."

Bergenville proved to be the old name of the township.

I then delicately told him that this was 1960. He seemed puzzled, to say the least.

"In 1756 I was sixty-five years old. I am not 204 years older?"

At this point, the ghost recognized the women's clothing the medium was wearing, and tore at them. I explained how we were able to "talk" to him. He seemed pacified.

"You'll accept my maize, my wine, my whiskey. . . ."

I discovered that maize and wine staples were the mainstays of the area at that period. I also found that Indian wars on a small scale were still common in this area in the middle 1700s. Moreover, the ghost referred to the "gate" as being in the *rear* of the house. This proved to be correct, for what is now the back of the house was then its front, facing the road.

Suddenly the ghost withdrew and after a moment another person, a woman, took over the medium. She complained bitterly that the Indians had taken one of her children, whose names she kept rattling off. Then she too withdrew, and Mrs. Meyers returned to her own body, none the worse for her experiences, none of which, incidentally, she remembered.

Shortly afterward, we returned to New York. It was as if

we had just come from another world. Leaving the poplar-lined road behind us, we gradually re-entered the world of gasoline and dirt that is the modern city.

Nothing further has been reported from the house in Bergen County, but I am sure the ghost, whom Mrs. B. had asked to stay as long as he wished, is still there. There is of course now no further need to bang doors, to call attention to his lonely self. *They know he is there with them.*

THE
FIFTH AVENUE
GHOST

S ome cases of haunted houses require but a single visit
to obtain information and evidence, others require
two or three. But very few cases in the annals of psychic research can equal or better the record set by the case
I shall call The Fifth Avenue Ghost. Seventeen sessions,
stretching over a period of five months, were needed to complete this most unusual case. I am presenting it here just
as it unfolded for us. I am quoting from our transcripts, our
records taken during each and every session; and because
so much evidence was obtained in this instance that could
only be obtained from the person these events actually happened to, it is to my mind a very strong case for the truth
about the nature of hauntings.

It isn't very often that one finds a haunted apartment listed
in the leading evening paper.

Occasionally, an enterprising real-estate agent will add the epithet "looks haunted" to a cottage in the country to attract the romanticist from the big city.

But the haunted apartment I found listed in the New York *Daily News* one day in July 1953 was the real McCoy. Danton Walker, the late Broadway columnist, had this item—

"One for the books: an explorer, advertising his Fifth Avenue Studio for sub-let, includes among the attractions 'attic dark room with ghost.'"

The enterprising gentleman thus advertising his apartment for rent turned out to be Captain Davis, a celebrated explorer and author of many books, including, here and there, some ghost lore. Captain Davis was no skeptic. To the contrary, I found him sincere and well aware of the existence of psychical research. Within hours, I had discussed the case with the *study group* which met weekly at the headquarters of the Association for Research and Enlightenment, the Edgar Cayce Foundation. A team was organized, consisting of Bernard Axelrod, Nelson Welsh, Stanley Goldberg and myself, and, of course, Mrs. Meyers as the medium. Bernard Axelrod and I knew that there was some kind of "ghost" at the Fifth Avenue address, but little more. The medium knew nothing whatever. Two days *after* the initial session, a somewhat fictional piece appeared in the *New York Times* (July 13, 1953) by the late Meyer Berger, who had evidently interviewed the *host*, but not the *ghost*. Mr. Berger quoted Captain Davis as saying there was a green ghost who had hanged himself from the studio gallery, and allegedly sticks an equally green hand out of the attic window now and then.

Captain Davis had no idea who the ghost was. This piece, it must be re-emphasized, appeared two days *after* the initial sitting at the Fifth Avenue house, and its contents were of course unknown to all concerned at the time.

In order to shake hands with the good Captain, we had to climb six flights of stairs to the very top of 226 Fifth Avenue. The building itself is one of those big old town houses popular in the mid-Victorian age, somber, sturdy, and well up to keeping its dark secrets behind its thickset stone walls. Captain Davis volunteered the information that previous tenants had included Richard Harding Davis, actor Richard Mansfield, and a lady magazine editor. Only the lady was still around and, when interviewed, was found to be totally ignorant of the entire ghost tradition, nor had she ever been disturbed. Captain Davis also told of guests in the house having seen the ghost at various times, though he himself had not. His home is one of the those fantastic and colorful apartments only an explorer or collector would own—a mixture of comfortable studio and museum, full of excitement and personality, and offering more than a touch of the Unseen. Two wild jungle cats completed the atmospheric picture, somewhat anticlimaxed by the host's tape recorder set up on the floor. The apartment is a kind of duplex, with a gallery or balcony jutting out into the main room. In the middle of this balcony was the window referred to in the

Times interview. Present were the host, Captain Davis, Mr. and Mrs. Bertram Long, the Countess de Sales, all friends of the host's, and the group of researchers previously mentioned—a total of eight people, and, if you wish, two cats. As with most sittings, tape recordings were made of the proceedings from beginning to end, in addition to which written notes were taken.

MEETING A GHOST

Like a well-rehearsed television thriller, the big clock in the tower across the square struck nine, and the lights were doused, except for one medium-bright electric lamp. This was sufficient light, however, to distinguish the outlines of most of the sitters, and particularly the center of the room around the medium.

A comfortable chair was placed under the gallery, in which the medium took her place; around her, forming a circle, sat the others, with the host operating the recorder and facing the medium. It was very still, and the atmosphere seemed tense. The medium had hardly touched the chair when she grabbed her own neck in the unmistakable manner of someone being choked to death, and nervously told of being "hung by the neck until dead." She then sat in the chair and Bernard Axelrod, an experienced hypnotist, conditioned her into her usual trance condition, which came within a few minutes.

With bated breath, we awaited the arrival of whatever

personality might be the "ghost" referred to. We expected some violence and, as will be seen shortly, we got it. This is quite normal with such cases, especially at the first contact. It appears that a "disturbed personality" continuously relives his or her "passing condition," or cause of death, and it is this last agony that so frequently makes ghostly visitations matters of horror. If emotional anxiety is the cause of death, or was present at death, then the "disturbed personality," or entity, will keep reliving that final agony, much like a phonograph needle stuck in the last groove of a record. But here is what happened on that first occasion.

Sitting of July 11th, 1953, at 226 Fifth Avenue

The medium, now possessed by unknown entity, has difficulty in speaking. Entity breaks into mad laughter full of hatred.

Entity: . . . curry the horse . . . they're coming . . . curry the horse! Where is Mignon? WHERE IS SHE?

Question: We wish to help you. Who is Mignon?
Entity: She should be here . . . where is she . . . you've got her! Where is she? Where is the baby?

Question: What baby?
Entity: What did they do with her?

Question: We're your friends.

Entity: (in tears) Oh, an enemy . . . an enemy. . . .

Question: What is your name?

Entity: Guychone . . . Guychone. . . . (expresses pain at the neck; hands feeling around are apparently puzzled by finding a woman's body)

Question: You are using someone else's body. (Entity clutches throat.) Does it hurt you there?

Entity: Not any more . . . it's whole again . . . I can't see. . . . All is so different, all is very strange . . . nothing is the same.

I asked how he died. This excited him immediately.

Entity: (hysterical) I didn't do it . . . I tell you I didn't do it, no . . . Mignon, Mignon . . . where is she? They took the baby . . . she put me away . . . they took her. . . . (Why did she put you away?) So no one could find me (Where?) I stay there (meaning upstairs) all the time.

At this point, tapes were changed. *Entity* asked where he came from, says Charleston, and that he lived in a white house.

Question: Do you find it difficult to use this body?

Entity: WHAT?? WHAT?? I'm HERE . . . I'm here. . . . This is my house . . . what are YOU doing here?

Question: **Tell me about the little room upstairs.**
Entity: (crying) Can I go . . . away . . . from the room?

At this point, the entity left, and the medium's *control*, Albert, took over her body.

Albert: There is a very strong force here, and it has been a
    little difficult. This individual here suffered violence
    at the hands of several people. He was a Confederate
    and he was given up, hidden here, while they made
    their escape.

Question: **What rank did he hold?**
Albert: I believe that he had some rank. It is a little du-
    bious as to what he was.

Question: **What was his name?**
Albert: It is not as he says. That is an assumed name, that
    he likes to take. He is not as yet willing to give full
    particulars. He is a violent soul underneath when he
    has opportunity to come, but he hasn't done damage to
    anyone, and we are going to work with him, if possible,
    from this side.

Question: **What about Mignon and the baby?**
Albert: Well, they of course are a long time *on this side*,
    but he never knew that, what became of them.
    They were separated cruelly. She did *not* do anything
    to him.

Question: **How did he leave this world?**

Albert: By violence. (Was he hanged?) Yes. (In the little room?) Yes. (Was it suicide or murder?) He says it was murder.

The *control* then suggests to end the trance, and try for results in "open" sitting. We slowly awaken the medium.

While the medium is resting, sitter Stanley Goldberg remarks that he has the impression that Guychone's father came from Scotland.

Captain Davis observes that at the exact moment of "frequency change" in the medium, that is, when Guychone left and Albert took over, the control light of the recording apparatus suddenly blazed up *of its own accord*, and had to be turned down by him.

A standing circle was then formed by all present, holding hands, and taking the center of the room. Soon the medium started swinging forward and back like a suspended body. She remarked feeling very stiff "from hanging and surprised to find that I'm whole, having been cut open in the middle."

Both Axelrod and I observed a luminescent white and *greenish* glow covering the medium, creating the impression of an older man without hair, with high cheekbones and thin arms. This was during the period when Guychone was speaking through the medium.

The seance ended at twelve-thirty. The medium reported feeling exhausted, with continued discomfort in the throat and stomach.

THE INVESTIGATION CONTINUES

Captain Davis, unfortunately, left on a world-wide trip the same week, and the new tenant was uncooperative. I felt we should continue the investigation. Once you pry a "ghost" loose from his place of unhappy memories, he can sometimes be contacted elsewhere.

Thus, a second sitting took place at the headquarters of the study group, on West 16th Street. This was a small, normally-furnished room free of any particular atmosphere, and throughout this and all following sittings, subdued light was used, bright enough to see all facial expressions quite clearly. There was smoking and occasional talking in low voices, none of which ever disturbed the work. Before the second sitting, Mrs. Meyers remarked that Guychone had "followed her home" from the Fifth Avenue place, and twice appeared to her at night in a kind of "whitish halo," with an expression of frantic appeal in his eyes. Upon her admonition to be patient until the sitting, the apparition had vanished.

Sitting of July 14th, 1953, at 125 West 16th Street

Question: Do you know what year this is?
Guychone: 1873.

Question: No, it is 1953. Eighty years have gone by. You are no longer alive. Do you understand?

Guychone: Eighty years? EIGHTY YEARS? I'm not a hundred-ten years?

Question: No, you're not. You're forever young. Mignon is on your side, too. We have come to help you understand yourself. What happened in 1873?

Guychone: Nobody's goddamn business . . . mine . . . mine!

Question: All right, keep your secret then, but don't you want to see Mignon? Don't you want justice done? (mad, bitter laughter) Don't you believe in God? (more laughter) The fact you are here and are able to speak, doesn't that prove that there is hope for you? What happened in 1873? Remember the house on Fifth Avenue, the room upstairs, the horse to be curried?

Guychone: Riding, riding . . . find her . . . they took her away.

Question: Who took her away?

Guychone: YOU! (threatens to strike interrogator)

Question: No, we're your friends. Where can we find a record of your Army service? Is it true you were on a dangerous mission?

Guychone: Yes.

Question: In what capacity?

Guychone: That is my affair! I do not divulge my secrets. I am a gentleman, and my secrets die with me.

Question: Give us your rank.

Guychone: I was a Colonel.

Question: In what regiment?

Guychone: Two hundred and sixth.

Question: Were you infantry or cavalry?

Guychone: Cavalry.

Question: In the War Between the States?

Guychone: Yes.

Question: Where did you make your home before you came to New York?

Guychone: Charleston . . . Elm Street.

Question: What is your family name, Colonel?

Guychone: (crying) As a gentleman, I am yet not ready to give you that information . . . it's no use, I won't name it.

Question: You make it hard for us, but we will abide by your wishes.

Guychone: (relieved) I am very much obliged to you . . . for giving me the information that it is EIGHTY YEARS. Eighty years!

. . .

I explain about the house on Fifth Avenue, and that Guy-chone's "presence" had been felt from time to time. Again, I ask for his name.

(Apparently fumbling for paper, he is given paper and fountain pen; the latter seems to puzzle him at first, but he then writes in the artistic, stylized manner of the mid-Victorian age—"Edouard Guychone.")

Question: **Is your family of French extraction?**
Guychone: Yes.

Question: **Are you yourself French or were you born in this country?**
Guychone: In this country . . . Charleston.

Question: **Do you speak French?**
Guychone: No.

Question: **Is there anything you want us to do for you? Any unfinished business?**
Guychone: Eighty years makes a difference . . . I am a broken man . . . God bless you . . . Mignon . . . it is so dark, so dark. . . .

I explain the reason for his finding himself temporarily in a woman's body, and how his hatred had brought him back to the house on Fifth Avenue, instead of passing over to the "other side."

Guychone: (calmer) There IS a God?

I ask when was he born.

Guychone: (unsure) 1840 . . . 42 years old. . . .

This was the most dramatic of the sittings. The transcript cannot fully convey the tense situation existing between a violent, hate-inspired and God-denying personality fresh from the abyss of perennial darkness, and an interrogator trying calmly to bring light into a disturbed mind. Toward the end of the session, Guychone understood about God, and began to realize that much time had passed since his personal tragedy had befallen him. Actually, the method of "liberating" a "ghost" is no different from that used by a psychiatrist to free a flesh-and-blood person from obsessions or other personality disturbances. Both deal with the mind.

It became clear to me that many more sessions would be needed to clear up the case, since the entity was reluctant to tell all. This is not the case with most "ghosts," who generally welcome a chance to "spill" emotions pent up for long years of personal hell. Here, however, the return of reason also brought back the critical faculty of reasoning, and evaluating information. We had begun to liberate Guychone's soul, but we had not yet penetrated to his conscience. Much hatred, fear, and pride remained, and had to be removed, before the true personality could emerge.

Sitting of July 21st, 1953

Albert, the medium's control, spoke first.

Question: Have you found any information about his wife and child?

Albert: You understand that this is our moral code, that that which comes from the individual within voluntarily is his sacred development. That which he wishes to divulge makes his soul what it should eventually be.

I asked that he describe Guychone's appearance to us.

Albert: At the moment he is little developed from the moment of passing. He is still like his latter moments in life. But his figure was of slight build, tall . . . five feet nine or ten . . . his face is round, narrow at the chin, high at the cheekbones, the nose is rather prominent, the mouth rather wide . . . the forehead high, at the moment of death and for many years previous very little hair. The eyes set close to the nose.

Question: **Have you learned his *real* name?**

Albert: It is not his wish as yet. He will tell you, he will develop his soul through his confession. Here he is!

Guychone: (at first grimacing in pain) It is nice to come, but it is hell . . . I have seen the light. It was so dark.

Question: **Your name, sir?**

Guychone: I was a gentleman . . . my name was defiled. I cannot see it, I cannot hear it, let me take it, when it is going to be right. I have had to pay for it; she has paid her price. I have been so happy. I have moved about. I have learned to right wrongs. I have seen the light.

Question: **I am going to open your eyes now. Look at the calender before you, and tell me what is the date on it? (placing calendar)**

Guychone: Nineteen fifty-three. . . . (pointing at the tape recorder in motion) Wagon wheels!

Question: **Give us the name of one of your fellow officers in the war. Write it down.**

Guychone: I am a poor soul. . . . (writes: Mignon my wife . . . Guychone) Oh, my feet, oh my feet . . . they hurt me so now . . . they bleed . . . I have to always go backwards, backwards. What shall I do with my feet? They had no shoes . . . we walked over burning weed . . . they burned the weed. . . . (Who?) The Damyankees . . . I wake up, I see the burning

weed.... (Where? When?) I have to reach out, I
have so much to reach for, have patience with me,
I can only reach so far—I'll forget. I will tell you
everything.... (Where?) Georgia! Georgia! (Did you
fight under General Lee?) I fell under him. (Did
you die under him?) No, no.

Question: **Who was with you in the regiment?**

Guychone: Johnny Greenly ... it is like another world ...
Jerome Harvey. (Who was the surgeon?) I did not
see him. Horse doctors. (Who was your orderly?)
Walter ... my boy ... I can't tell the truth, and I try so
hard.... I will come with the truth when it comes, you
see the burning weeds came to me ... I will think of
happier things to tell ... I'd like to tell you about the
house in Charleston, on Elm Street. I think it is 320, I
was born in it.

Question: **Any others in the family?**

Guychone: Two brothers. They died. They were in the
war with me. I was the eldest. William, and Paul.
(And you're Edward?) Yes. (Your mother?) Mary.
(Your father?) Frederick. (Where was he born?)
Charleston. (Your mother's maiden name?) Ah ...!
(Where did you go to college?) William ... William
and ... a white house with green grass. (When did
you graduate?) Fifty-three ... ONE HUNDRED
YEARS.... It is hard to get into those corners where
I can't think any more.

"I never had my eyes open before, in trance," observed Mrs. Meyers afterwards. "While I could look at you and you looked like yourself, I could almost look through you. That never happened before. I could only see what I focused on. This machine . . . it seemed the wheels were going much, much *faster* than they are going now."

On July 25th, 1953, a "planchette" session was held at the home of Mrs. Meyers, with herself and the late Mrs. Zoe Britton present, during which Guychone made himself known, and stated that he had a living son, eighty-nine years old, now living in a place called Seymour, West Virginia.

EVIDENTIAL MATERIAL BEGINS TO PILE UP

By now we knew we had an unusual case. I went through all the available material on this period (and there is a lot), without turning up anyone named Guychone.

These were extremely hot afternoons, but the quest went on. Rarely has any psychic researcher undertaken a similarly protracted project to hunt down psychic evidence.

Sitting of July 28th, 1953

Finding a St. Michael's medal around my neck, Guychone says it reminds him of a medal of St. Anne, which his "Huguenot mother," Marie Guychone, had given him.

Question: Do you remember the name of your college?
Guychone: Two colleges. St. Anne's in Charleston,
    South Carolina. . . . Only one thought around
    another, that's all I had—curry the horses. Why?
    I know now. I remember. I want to say my mother
    is here, I saw her, she says God bless you. I
    understand more now. Thank you. Pray
    for me.

Sitting of August 4th, 1953

This sitting repeated previous information and consisted in a cat-and-mouse game between Guychone and myself. However, toward the end, Guychone began to speak of his son Gregory, naming him for the first time. He asked us to find him. We asked, "What name does Gregory use?" Guychone casually answered: "I don't know . . . Guy-chone . . . maybe McGowan. . . ." The name McGowan came very quietly, but sufficiently distinct to be heard by all present. At the time, we were not overwhelmed. Only when research started to yield results did we realize that it was his real name at last. But I was not immediately successful in locating McGowan on the regimental rosters, far from it! I was misled by his statement of having served in the cavalry, and naturally gave the cavalry rosters my special attention, but he wasn't in them. Late in August I went through the city records of Charleston, West Virginia, on a futile search for the Guychone family, assuming still that they were his in-laws. Here I found mention of a "McGowan's Brigade."

Sitting of August 18th, 1953

Question: **Please identify yourself, Colonel.**
McGowan: Yes . . . Edward . . . I can stay? I can stay?

Question: **Why do you want so much to stay? Are you not happy where you are?**
McGowan: Oh yes. But I like to talk very much . . . how happy I am.

Question: **What was your mother's name?**
McGowan: Marie Guychone.

Question: **What is your own name?**
McGowan: Guychone.

Question: Yes; that is the name you *used*, but you really are . . . ?

McGowan: Edward Mac . . . Mac . . . curry the horses! (excited, is calmed by me) Yes, I see . . . Mac . . . McGowan! I remember more now, but I can only tell what I know . . . it is like a wall . . . I remember a dark night, I was crazy . . . war on one hand, fighting, bullets . . . and then, flying away, chasing, chasing, chasing . . .

Question: What regiment were you with?

McGowan: Six . . . two . . . sometimes horse . . . oh, in that fire. . . .

Question: Who was your commanding general?

McGowan: But—Butler.

He then speaks of his service in two regiments, one of which was the Sixth South Carolina Regiment, and he mentions a stand on a hill, which was hell, with the Damyankees on all sides. He says it was at Chattanooga.

Question: The house on Fifth Avenue, New York . . . do you remember the name of your landlord?

McGowan: A woman . . . Elsie (or L. C.) . . . stout. . . .

Actually, he says, a man collected the rent, which he had trouble paying at times. He knew a man named Pat Duffy in New York. He was the man who worked for his landlady, collecting the rent, coming to his door.

During the interrogation about his landlord, McGowan suddenly returns to his war experiences. "There was a Griffin," he says, referring to an officer he knew.

Sitting of August 25th, 1953

"The Colonel," as we now called him, came through very clearly. He introduced himself by his true name. Asked again about the landlady in New York, he now adds that she was a *widow*. Again, he speaks of "Griff . . . Griff. . . ." Asked what school he went to, he says "St. Anne's College in Charleston, South Carolina, and also William and Mary College in Virginia, the latter in 1850, 51, 52, 53, 54." What was his birthday? He says "February 10, 1830." Did he write any official letters during the war? He says, "I wrote to General Robert E. Lee." What about? When? "January, 1864. Atlanta. . . . I needed horses, horses, wheels to run the things on." Did you get them? "No." What regiment was he with then? "The Sixth from South Carolina." But wasn't he from West Virginia? Amazed, McGowan says, "No, from South Carolina."

I then inquired about his family in New York.

McGowan explained that his mother did live with him there, and died there, but after his own death "they" went away, including his sister-in-law Gertrude and brother William. Again, he asks that we tell his son Gregory "that his father did *not* do away with himself."

I asked, "Where is there a true picture of you?" McGowan

replied, "There is one in the courthouse in Charleston, South Carolina." What kind of a picture? "Etch . . . etch . . . *tintype*!"

All through these sittings it was clear that McGowan's memory was best when "pictures" or scenes were asked for, and worst when precise names or dates were being requested. He was never sure when he gave a figure, but was very sure of his facts when he spoke of situations or relationships. Thus, he gave varying dates for his own birthday, making it clear that he was hazy about it, not even aware of having given discrepant information within a brief period.

But then, if a living person undergoes a severe shock, is he not extremely hazy about such familiar details as his name or address? Yet, most shock victims can *describe* their house, or their loved ones. The human memory, apparently, is more reliable in terms of associations, when under stress, than in terms of factual information, like names and figures.

By now research was in full swing, and it is fortunate for the sake of the Survival View that so much prima-facie evidence was obtained *before* the disclosure of McGowan's true name started the material flowing. Thus, the old and somewhat tiring argument of "mental telepathy" being responsible for some of the information, can only be applied, if at all, to a part of the sittings. No one can read facts in a mind *before* they get into that mind!

The sittings continued in weekly sessions, with Colonel McGowan rapidly becoming our "star" visitor.

Sitting of September 1st, 1953

Question: What was your rank at the end of the war?
McGowan: That was on paper . . . made to serve.

Question: Did you become a general?
McGowan: Naw . . . honors . . . I take empty honors. . . .

Question: When you went to school, what did you study?
McGowan: The law of the land.

Question: What happened at Manassas?
McGowan: Oh . . . defeat. Defeat.

Question: What happened to you personally at Manassas?
McGowan: Ah, cut, cut. Bayonets. Ah. Blood, blood.

Question: What happened at Malvern Hill?
McGowan: Success. We took the house. Low brick
    building. We wait. They come up and we see right
    in the mouth of a cannon. 1864. They burned the
    house around our ears. But we didn't move.

Question: What was under your command at that time?
McGowan: Two divisions.

Question: How many regiments?

McGowan: Four . . . forty . . . (Four?) TEEN!

Question: What did you command?

McGowan: My commander was shot down, I take over. (Who for?) John . . . Major. . . .

Question: Listen, Colonel, your name is not Edward. Is there any other first or middle name you used? (Silence) Did anyone of high rank serve from South Carolina? (My brother William.) Anyone else? (Paul.)

McGowan: Do you think of Charles McGowan? That was no relation of mine. He was on the waterfront. He was . . . exporter.

Question: Were you at Gettysburg, Colonel? (Yes.) What regiments were under your command then?

McGowan: I had a wound at Gettysburg. I was very torn. (Where did you get the wound?) Atlanta . . . change of rank. Empty honors. (About his son Gregory.) Seymour . . . many years Lowell, Massachusetts, and then he went back down South, Seymour, South Carolina, and sometimes West Virginia . . . he was in a store, he left and then he came into property, mother also had property, down there near Charleston in West Virginia . . . that is where he is, yes.

Question: You say your father was Frederick? (Yes.) Who was William? (My brother.) Who was Samuel? (Long pause, *stunned*, then: *I* wrote that name!) Why didn't you tell us? (Crying: I didn't want to tell. . . .) Tell us your true rank, too. (I don't care what it was). Please don't evade us. What was your rank? (Brigadier . . . General). Then you are General Samuel McGowan?

McGowan: You made me very unhappy . . . such a name (crying) . . . blood, empty honors. . . .

Question: Who was James Johnson? (My commander.) What happened to him? (Indicates he was shot.) Who took over for Johnson? (I did.) What regiment was it?

McGowan: I don't know the figures . . . I don't know.

Question: Your relative in New York, what was his name?

McGowan: Peter Paul.

Question: What was his profession?

McGowan: A doctor. (Any particular kind of doctor?) Cuts. (What kind?) (McGowan points to face.) (Nose doctor?) (McGowan points to mouth and shakes head.) (Mouth doctor?) (McGowan violently grabs his teeth and shakes them.) (Oh, teeth? A dentist.) (McGowan nods assent.)

Question: I will name some regiments, tell me if any of them mean anything to you. The 10th . . . the 34th . . . the 14th. . . . (McGowan reacts.) The 14th? Does it mean anything to you?

McGowan: I don't know, figures don't mean anything on this side. . . .

SOME INTERESTING FACTS BROUGHT OUT BY RESEARCH

In the sitting of August 18th, McGowan stated his land-lord was a woman and that her name was "Elsie" or L. C. *The Hall of Records* of New York City lists the owner of 226 Fifth Avenue as "Isabella S. Clarke, from 1853 to (at least) March 1, 1871." In the same sitting, McGowan stated that Pat Duffy was the man who actually came to collect the rent, working for the landlady. Several days *after* this information was *voluntarily* received from the entity, I found in *Trow's New York City Directory for 1869/70*:

> Page 195: "Clark, Isabella, wid. Constantine h. (house) 45 Cherry."
>
> Page 309: "Duffy, Patrick, laborer, 45 Cherry."
>
> This could be known only to someone who actually *knew* these people, eighty years ago; it proved our ghost was *there* in 1873!
>
> The sitting of September 1st also proved fruitful.
>
> A "Peter McGowan, dentist, 253 W. 13 St." appears in *Trow's New York City Directory for 1870/71*.
>
> J. F. J. Caldwell, in his *History of a Brigade of South Carolinians known first as "Gregg's," and subsequently as "McGowan's Brigade"* (Philadelphia, 1866), reports:
>
> Page 10: "The 14th Regiment South Carolina Volunteers selected for field officers . . . Col. James Jones, *Lt. Col. Samuel McGowan* . . . (1861)."

Page 12: "Colonel Samuel McGowan commands the 14th Regiment."

Page 18: "McGowan arrives from the Chickahominy River (under Lee)."

Page 24: "Conspicuous gallantry in the battle of Malvern Hill."

Page 37: "... of the 11 field officers of our brigade, seven were wounded: Col. McGowan, etc. (in the 2nd battle of Manassas)."

Page 53: "Col. Samuel McGowan of the 14th Regiment (at Fredericksburg)."

Page 60: "The 13th and 14th regiments under McGowan...."

Page 61: "Gen. Gregg's death Dec. 14, 1862. McGowan succeeds to command."

Page 66: "Biography: Born Laurens district, S.C. 1820. Graduated 1841 South Carolina College, Law; in Mexican War, then settled as lawyer in Abbeville, S.C. Became a Brig. Gen. January 20, 1863, assists in taking Ft. Sumter April 1861; but lapsing commission as General in State Militia, he becomes Lt. Col. in the Confederate Army, takes part at Bull Run, Manassas Plains, under Gen. Bonham. Then elected Lt. Col. of 14th Regiment, S.C.; Spring 1862, made full Col. *succeeding Col. Jones who was killed*. McGowan is *wounded* in battle of Manassas." Biographer Caldwell, who was McGowan's aide as a lieutenant, says (in 1866) "he still lives."

Page 79. "April 29, 1863, McGowan's *Brigade* gets orders to be ready to march. Gen. McGowan commands the brigade."

Page 80: "Wounded again (Fredericksburg)."

Page 89: "Gen. Lee reviews troops including McGowan's. Brigade now consists of 1st, 12th, 13th, 14th Regiments and Orr's Rifles. Also known as 'McGowan's Sharpshooters.'"

Page 91: "McGowan takes part in battle of Chancellorsville."

Page 96: "Battle of Gettysburg: McGowan commands 13th, 12th, 14th, and 1st."

Page 110: "McGowan near Culpepper Courthouse."

Page 22: "Gen. McGowan returned to us in February (1864). He had not sufficiently recovered from the wound received at Chancellorsville to walk well, but remained with us and discharged all the duties of his office."

Page 125: *About Butler:* "Butler to lead column (against McGowan) from the Eastern coast." Another Butler (Col.) commanded the Confederate 1st Regt. (Battle of Chickamauga)

Page 126sq.: "Battle of Spottsylvania, May 1864."

Page 133: "Gen. Lee and Gen. Hill were there (defeat)."

Page 142: "McGowan wounded by a 'minie ball,' in the right arm, quits field."

But to continue with our sittings, and with McGowan's personal recollections—

Sitting of September 8th, 1953

♆

McGowan: (speaking again of his death) "It was in the forties . . . they killed me on the top floor. They dragged me
up, that 'man of color' named Walter. He was a giant of a
man. She was a virtuous woman, I tell you she was. But they
would not believe it."

I wanted to get his reaction to a name I had found in the
records, so I asked, "Have you ever met a McWilliams?"

McGowan: You have the knowledge of the devil with you.
 Her family name.

Question: **Did you stay in New York until your passing?**
McGowan: 1869, 1873. Back and forth. I have written
 to Lee, Jackson, James, and Beaufort. 1862–63, March.

Question: **What did you do at the end of the war?**
McGowan: Back and forth, always on the go. Property was
 gone, ruined. Plantations burned. I did not work. I
 could not. Three or four bad years. I quit. My wits, my
 wits. My uncle. The house was burned in Charleston.
 Sometimes Columbia. (Then, of Mignon, his wife, he
 says.) She died in 1892 . . . Francois Guychone . . .
 he was so good to little boys, he made excursions in the
 Bay of Charleston—we sailed in boats. He was my uncle.

Sitting of September 15th, 1953

I asked, what did he look like in his prime.

McGowan: I wasn't too bad to look at, very good brow,
   face to the long, and at one time I indulged in the
   whiskers . . . not so long, for the chin . . . colonial . . . I
   liked to see my chin a good deal, sometimes I cover
   (indicates mustache) . . . .

Question: **What can you tell us about the cemetery in
   Abbeville?**
McGowan: There is a monument, the family cemetery . . .
   nobody cared . . . my father was born the fifth of
   January. . . . (What was on your tombstone?)
   Samuel Edward McGowan, born . . . 32? . . . died
   1883? 1873? 1–8–7 hard to read, so dirty . . . age
   40 . . . 41 . . . gray-brown stars . . . battered. . . . I go
   between the bushes, I look at the monument, it's
   defaced. . . .

Question: **What news did your family give out of your
   death?**
McGowan: Foul play. (What happened to the
   body?) Cremated I guess, I think in this city.
   The remains were destroyed: not in the grave, a
   monument to a memory. . . . (What did they tell the

public?) Lost forever . . . I could have been at sea . . .
house was destroyed by fire. . . . (Do you mean
there is no official record of your death?) No. *Not
identical to* passing, they never told the exact month
or day . . . I see . . . 1879 . . . very blurred . . . September
4th. . . .

Question: **Were you ever injured in an argument?**
McGowan: I spent much time on my back because of a
wound . . . on my head. (An argument?) Yes. (With
whom?) A man. Hand to hand. Rapier. . . . Glen,
Glen . . . Ardmore.

Sitting of September 22nd, 1953

"Mother" Marie Guychone spoke briefly in French and was
followed by McGowan. He said he was at one time "An Associate Justice" in the city of Columbia.

Here again do I wish to report some more research information bearing on this part of the investigation. Evans,
in his *Confederate Military History*, 1899*, has a picture of
the General which became available to us *after* the September 22nd sitting. His biography, on page 414, mentions
the fact that "he was associate Justice of the (State) Supreme
Court." Curiously, this author also states that McGowan

---

* Vol. V., p. 409.

died in "December 1893." Careful scrutiny of two major
New York dailies then existing (*Post* and *Times*) brought to
light that the author of the *Confederate Military History*
made a mistake, albeit an understandable one. A certain
Ned McGowan, described as a "notorious character, aged
80" had died in San Francisco on December 9, 1893. This
man was also a Confederate hero. (*The New York Times*,
XII/9). However, the same source (*The New York Times*,
August 13, 1897) reports General McGowan's death as having occurred on the ninth of August, *1897*. The obituary
contains the facts already noted in the biography quoted
earlier, plus one interesting additional detail, that McGowan
received a cut across the scalp in a duel.

Another good source, *The Dictionary of American Biography*, says of our subject: "*McGowan, Samuel*. Son of William and Jeannie McGowan, law partner of William H.
Parker. Died August 9, 1897 in Abbeville. Buried in Long
Cane Cemetery in Abbeville. Born Oct. 9, 1819 in Crosshill
section of Laurens district, S.C. *Mother's name was Mc-
Williams*. Law partner of *Perrin* in Abbeville. Representative in State House of South Carolina. Elected to Congress,
but not seated."

A Colonel at Gettysburg, by Varina Brown, about her
late husband Colonel Brown, contains the following: "In
the battle of Jericho Mills, '*Griffin's Division*' of Federals
wrought havoc against McGowan's Brigade."

Correspondence with Mrs. William Gaynes, a resident of
Abbeville, revealed on October 1st, 1953—"The old general

was a *victim of the failing mind* but he was doctored up until the date of his death. He was attended by his cousin *Dr. F. E. Harrison.*"

Eminent & Representative Men of South Carolina by Brant & Fuller (Madison, Wisconsin, 1892) gives this picture:

"Samuel McGowan was born of *Scotch* Irish parents in Laurens County, S.C., on October 9th, 1819. Graduated with distinction from the South Carolina College in 1841. Read law at Abbeville with T. C. Perrin who offered him a partnership. He entered the service as a private and went to Mexico with the Palmetto Regiment. He was appointed on the general Quartermaster's Staff with the rank of Captain. After the war he returned to Abbeville and resumed the practice of Law with T. C. Perrin. He married Susan Caroline, eldest daughter of Judge David Lewis Wardlaw and they lived in Abbeville until some years after the death of Gen. McGowan in 1897. The home of Gen. McGowan still stands in Abbeville and was sold some time ago to the Baptist Church for 50,000 dollars.... After the war he entered law practice with William H. Parker (1869/1879) *in Abbeville*. He took an interest in political affairs ... member of the Convention that met in Columbia in September, 1865. Elected to Congress but not allowed to take his seat. Counted out on the second election two years later. In 1878 he was a member of the State Legislature and in 1879 he was elected Associate Justice of the State Supreme Court.

"General McGowan lived a long and honorable life in

Abbeville. He was a contributing member of the Episcopal Church, Trinity, and became a member later in life. At his death the following appeared in the *Abbeville Medium*, edited by Gen. R. R. Hemphill who had served in Mc-Gowan's Brigade. 'General Samuel McGowan *died at his home in this city* at 8:35 o'clock last Monday morning August 8th. Full of years and honors he passed away surrounded by his family and friends. He had been in declining health for some time and suffered intense pain, though his final sickness was for a few days only and at the end all was Peace. Impressive services were held in *Trinity Church* Tuesday afternoon, at four o'clock, the procession starting from the residence. At the Church, the procession . . . preceded by Dr. Wm. M. Grier and Bishop Ellison Capers who read the solemn service . . . directly behind the coffin old Daddy Willis Marshall, a colored man who had served him well, bore a laurel wreath. Gen. McGowan was buried at *Long Lane* cemetery and there is a handsome stone on the plot."

Mrs. William Gaynes further reports:

"Gen. McGowan had a 'fine line of profanity' and used it frequently in Court. He was engaged in a duel once with Col. John *Cunningham* and was wounded behind one ear and came near passing out. Col. Cunningham challenged Col. *Perrin who refused* the challenge on the ground that he did not approve of dueling, and Gen. McGowan took up the challenge and the duel took place at Sand Bar Ferry, near Augusta, with McGowan being wounded.

"As far as I know, there was never any difficulty between Mrs. McGowan and the old General. His father-in-law, Judge Wardlaw, married *Sarah* Rebecca Allen, and *her* mother was Mary Lucia Garvey."

In other words, Judge Wardlaw married *Sarah Garvey*.

Mrs. Gaynes continues: "I have seen him frequently on his way to his law office, for he had to pass right by *our* office. If he ever was out of town for any length of time, Abbeville *did not know it.*"

The inscription on Samuel McGowan's tombstone in Long Cane Graveyard reads as follows:

"Samuel McGowan, born Laurens County 9 October 1819. Died in Abbeville 9 August 1897. Go soldier to thy honored rest, thy trust and honor valor bearing. The brave are the tenderest, the loving are the daring."

Side 2: "From humble birth he rose to the highest honor in Civic and military life. A patriot and a leader of men. In peace his country called him, he waited not to her call in war. A man's strength, a woman's tenderness, a child's simplicity were his and his a heart of charity fulfilling the law of love. He did good and not evil all the days of his life and at its end his country his children and his children's children rise up and call him blessed. In Mexican War 1846–1848. A Captain in United States Army. The Confederate War 1861–1865. A Brigadier General C.S.A. Member of the Legislature 1848–1850. Elected to Congress 1866. Associate Justice of Supreme Court of South Carolina 1878–1894. A hero in two wars. Seven times wounded. A leader at the Bar, a wise law giver a righteous judge. He rests from his labors and his works do follow him."

MCGOWAN BECOMES
A "REGULAR" OF THE
WEEKLY SITTINGS

General McGowan had by now become an always impatient weekly "guest" at our sittings, and he never liked the idea of leaving. Whenever it was suggested that time was running short, McGowan tried to prolong his stay by becoming suddenly very talkative.

Sitting of September 29th, 1953

A prepared list of eight names, all fictitious but one (the sixth is that of Susan Wardlaw, McGowan's wife) is read to him several times. McGowan reacts to two of the non-existent names, but not to the one of his wife. One of the fictitious names is John D. Sumter, to which McGowan mumbles, "Colonel." Fact is, there *was* a Colonel Sumter in the Confederate Army!

McGowan also described in detail the farm where his son Gregory now lives. Asked about the name Guychone, he says it comes from Louisiana; Mignon, on her mother's side, had it. He identifies his hometown newspapers as "Star-Press." ("*Star-Press*, paper, picture, Judge, Columbia, picture in paper. . . . ")

Question: **Who was Dr. Harrison?**
McGowan: Family doctor.

Question: **Is your home in Abbeville still standing?**
McGowan: It isn't *what it was*. Strange pictures and
    things. (Anyone live in it?) No. Strange things, guns
    and cannons.

Sitting of October 14th, 1953

McGowan says he had two daughters. Trying again to read
his tombstone, he says, "1887, or is it 97?" As to his birth-
year, he reads, "1821. . . . 31?"

Sitting of October 20th, 1953

When the control introduces McGowan, there is for several
moments intense panic and fear brought on by a metal
necklace worn by the medium. When McGowan is assured
that there is no longer any "rope around his neck," he calms
down, and excuses himself for his regression.

Question: **Who was the Susan you mentioned the last
    time?**
McGowan: The mother of my children.

Question: What was her other name?
McGowan: Cornelia.

Question: Were you elected to Congress?
McGowan: What kind of Congress? (The U. S. Congress.)
   I lost. Such a business, everybody grabs, everybody
   steals. . . . Somebody always buys the votes and it's such
   a mess.

Question: Are Mignon and Susan one and the same
   person or not?
McGowan: I don't wish to commit myself. (I insist.) They
   are *not*!

Question: Let us talk about Susan. What profession did
   your father-in-law follow?
McGowan: Big man . . . in the law.

Question: What was your mother-in-law's first name?
McGowan: Sarah.

Question: Did she have another name?
McGowan: Garfey. . . .

Question: Coffee? Spell it.
McGowan: Not coffee. *Garvey!*

. . .

At a sitting on October 28th, 1953, at the home of Mrs. Meyers, McGowan's alleged grandson, Billy, manifested himself as follows:

"My name is William, I passed in 1949, at Charleston. I'm a grandson of General McGowan. I was born in Abbeville, January 2nd, 1894. Gregory is half-brother, son of the French bitch. He (McGowan) would have married her, but he had a boss, grandfather, who held the purse strings. Susan's father of Dutch blood, hard-headed."

Sitting of October 29th, 1953

♆

McGowan: You must find Gregory. He may be surprised about his father, but I must let him know I wanted for him, and they took for *them* . . . all. And they gave him nothing. Nothing! I had made other plans. (Was there a will?) There was . . . but I had a Judge in the family that made other plans . . . THEY WERE NOT MINE! You must tell Gregory I provided. . . . I tell you only the truth because I was an honest man . . . I did the best for my family, for my people, for those I considered my countrymen, that what you now call posterity . . . I suffer my own sins. . . . For you maybe it means nothing, for me, for those who remember me, pity . . . they are now aware of the truth, only now is my son unaware of the truth. Sir, you are my best friend. And I go into hell for you. I tell you always the truth, Sir, but there are things that would not concern you or anybody. But I will give you those names yet!

Question: **I ask again for the name of McGowan's father-in-law.**
McGowan: Wida . . . Wider.

THE "GHOST" IS FREED

One of the functions of a "rescue circle" is to make sure a disturbed entity does not return to the scene of his unhappiness. This mission was accomplished here.

Sitting of November 3rd, 1953

McGowan: I see the house where I lived, you know, where you found me. *I go there now, but I am not anymore disturbed.* I found my mother and my father. They could not touch me, but *now*, we touch hands. I live over my life, come back to many things. Herman! He was a good soul, he helped me when I was down in Atlanta. He bathed my feet, my legs were scorched, and he was good to me, and he is over here. I thank him. I thanked him then, but I was the big man, and he was nothing, but now I see he is a fine gentleman, he polished my boots, he put my uniform in order.

Sitting of November 6th, 1953

꓿

I was alone with the medium, Mrs. Meyers, at her home, when I had a chance to question McGowan about his apparent murder, and the "conspiracy of silence" concerning it.

McGowan: The Judge protected them, did not report my death. They had devised the kidnapping. I was murdered downstairs, strangled by the kidnapper Walter. He took her (Mignon) all the way to Boston. I wore the uniform of Damyankees (during the war), rode a horse *every night* to Boston . . . no, I made a mistake. I came to my Uncle Peter Paul in New York, I had a letter from Marie Guychone, she was in New York. Begged me to find Mignon and Gregory. I come to New York. I can't find her, she was in Boston then, but I didn't know that until later. Marie Guychone remained with my uncle, and I gave up the chase, and like a thief crawled back to Confederate grounds. That was in 1863. After the war, there was a struggle, property was worthless, finally the Union granted that we withdraw our holdings, and with that I came to New York. My mother and father came also, until rehabilitation was sufficient for their return.

    I continued to live with my wife, Susan, and the children, and I found Mignon. She had escaped, and came to her mother in New York. I made a place for them to live with my uncle and when my wife returned to stay with her father (the Judge), I had Mignon, but she was pregnant and she didn't know it, and there was a black child—there was unpleasantness between us, I didn't know if it were mine and Mignon was black, but it was not so, it was his child (Walter's), and he came for it and for her, he traced her to my house (on Fifth Avenue); my father-in-law (the Judge) was the informer, and he (Walter) strangled me, he was a big man.

And when I was not dead yet, he dragged me up the stairs. Mignon was not present, not guilty. I think . . . it was in January 1874. But I may be mistaken about time. Gregory had two sons, William and Edward. William died on a boat in the English Channel in 1918. Gregory used the name *Fogarty*, not McGowan. The little black boy died, they say. It was just as well for him.

McGowan then left peacefully, promising more information about the time lag between his given date and that officially recorded. I told him the difference was "about twenty years." For the first time, McGowan had stated his story reasonably, although some details of it would be hard to check. No murder or suicide was reported in the newspapers of the period, similar to this case. But of course anyone planning a crime like this might have succeeded in keeping it out of the public eye. We decided to continue our sittings.

Sitting of November 10th, 1953

McGowan talked about the duel he fought, which cost him his hair, due to a wound on the left side, back and top of his head. It was over a woman and against a certain Colonel C., something like "Collins," but a longer name. He said that Perry or Perrin *did so* make a stand, as if someone had doubted it!

MORE PROOF TURNS UP!

Leading away from personal subjects, the questioning now proceeded toward matters of general interest about New York at the time of McGowan's residence here. The advantage of this line of questioning is its neutral value for research purposes; and as *no research* was undertaken until after the sittings of November 17th, mental telepathy must be excluded as an alternate explanation!

Sitting of November 17th, 1953

McGowan: You don't have a beard. They called them *milksops* in my days, the beardless boys!

Question: **What did they call a man who was a nice dresser and liked ladies?**

McGowan: A Beau Brummel.

Question: **What did they call a gentleman who dressed too well, too fancifully?**

McGowan: A fop.

Question: **What was your favorite sport?**

McGowan: Billiards (He explains he was good at it, and the balls were *made of cloth*.)

Question: **What was the favorite game of your day?**

McGowan: They played a *Cricket* kind of game. . . .

Question: **Who was mayor of New York?**

McGowan: Oh . . . Grace. Grace . . . *Edmond* . . . Grace . . . something like it.

William R. Grace was mayor of New York, 1881–1882, and Franklin Edson (not Edmond) followed, 1883–1884. Also, plastic billiard balls as we know them today are a comparatively recent invention, and billiard balls in the Victorian era were indeed made of cloth. The cricket kind of game must be baseball. Beau Brummel, fop, milksop are all authentic Victorian expressions.

Sitting of November 26th, 1953

I asked the General about trains in New York in his time.

McGowan: They were smoke stacks, up in the air,
smoke got in your eyes, they went down to the Globe
Building near City Hall. The *Globe* Building was near
Broadway and Nassau. The train went up to Harlem.
It was a *nice* neighborhood. I took many strolls in
the park.

Question: **Where was the Hotel Waldorf-Astoria?**
McGowan: Near Fifth Avenue and 33rd, near my house . . .
and the Hotel Prince George. Restaurants were Ye
Olde Southern, Hotel Brevoort. You crack my
brain, you are worse than that boss in the Big
House, Mr. Tammany and Mr. Tweed. (I discussed
his house, and he mentioned doing business
with—) Somebody named *Costi* . . . I paid $128.50
a month for the entire house. A suit of clothes cost
$100.00.

Question: **Who lived next door to you?**
McGowan: Herman . . . *was a carriage smith.* He had a
business where he made carriages. He lived next door,
but his business was not there, the shop was on Third
Avenue, Third Street, near the river.

Question: Any other neighbors?

McGowan: Corrigan Brown, *a lawyer* . . . lived three
houses down. The editor of the *Globe* was White . . .
Stone . . . White . . . the editor of the *Globe* was not
good friends with the man in the Big House. They
broke his house down when he lived on Fifth Avenue.
He was a neighbor. Herman the carriage maker made
good carriages. I bought one with fringes and two
seats, a cabrio. . . .

Question: Did you have a janitor?

McGowan: There was a black boy named Ted, mainly colored servants, we had a gardener, white, named Patrick.
He collects the rent, he lives with the Old Crow on
Cherry Street. Herman lives next door. He had a long
mustache and square beard. He wore a frock coat, a dia-
mond tie pin, and spectacles. I never called him Herman . . . (trying to remember his true name) . . . Gray . . .
I never called him Herman. He had a wife named
Birdie. His wife had a sister named Finny who lived
there too . . . Mrs. Finny . . . she was a young widow with
two children . . . she was a good friend to my Susan.

McGowan then reluctantly signs his name as requested.
Research, undertaken *after* the sitting, again excluded
mental telepathy. The facts were of a kind not likely to be
found in the records, *unless* one were specifically looking
for them!

The *New York Globe* building, which McGowan remembers "near Broadway and Nassau," was then (1873) at 7 Spruce Street and apparently also at 162 Nassau Street.* The *Globe* is on Spruce, and *Globe and Evening Press* on Nassau, around the corner.

McGowan describes the steam-powered elevated railroad that went from City Hall to Harlem. Steam cars started in 1867 and ran until 1906, according to the New York Historical Society, and there were two lines fitting his description, "Harlem, From Park Row to . . . E. 86th Street" and "Third Avenue, from Ann Street through Park Row to . . . Harlem Bridge."†

McGowan was right in describing Harlem as a nice neighborhood in his day. Harlem did not become a low-rent, colored section until the present century.

McGowan also acknowledged at once that he had been to the Waldorf-Astoria, and correctly identified its position at Fifth Avenue and 33rd Street. The Waldorf-Astoria came into being on March 14th, 1893. Consequently, McGowan *was alive then*, and evidently sane, if he could visit such places as the Waldorf, Brevoort, and others.

McGowan refers to a (later) landlord as Costi. In 1895, a real-estate firm by the name of George and John Coster was situated at 173 Fifth Avenue, a few houses down the street from McGowan's place.‡

As for the carriage smith named Herman, a little later

---

* *Trow's New York City Directory for 1872/73*, p. 448, regular section and p. 38, City Register section.
† *Ibid.*, City Register, p. 18, under "City Railroads."
‡ *Trow*, 1895/96, p. 550.

referred to as Herman Gray, there was a carriage maker
named William H. Gray from 1872 or earlier, and existing
beyond the turn of the century, whose shop was at first at
20 Wooster Street,* and who lived at 258 West Fourth
Street, until at least 1882. In 1895 he is listed as living at 275
West 94th Street. Not all Trow volumes in between are
available, so that residence in McGowan's neighborhood
can neither be confirmed nor denied. At one time, Gray's
shops were on West Broadway. As for Corrigan Brown, the
lawyer neighbor, McGowan's mispronouncing of names
almost tripped me up. There was no such lawyer. There
was, however, one Edmond Congar Brown, lawyer, listed
for the first time as such in 1886, and before that only as
a clerk. No home is, unfortunately, listed for his later
years.† McGowan stated that the editor of the *Globe* was
named White-and-something, and that he lived near his
(McGowan's) house on Fifth Avenue.

Well, one Horace P. Whitney, editor, business, 128 Fulton Street, home, 287 Fifth Avenue, is listed in Trow.‡ And
128 Fulton Street is the place of the *Globe*'s competitor, the
New York Mercury, published by Cauldwell and Whitney.§

That McGowan did not die in 1873 seems certain to me, as
the above information proves. But if he did not die in 1873,

---

* *Trow*, 1872/73, City Register, p. 27.
† *Trow*, 1895/96, p. 174, lists his office as 132 Nassau.
‡ 1872, p. 1287, regular section.
§ *Trow*, 1872, City Register section, p. 39.

something very traumatic must have been done to him at that time. Or perhaps the murder, if such it was, took place in 1897?

It could well be that General McGowan will take this ultimate secret with him into the Great Land where he now dwells safely forever.

GOOD MEDIUMS
ARE RARE

B y now my readers must realize that a ghost hunt is nothing without a good medium. True, occasionally apparitions materialize to outsiders without, apparently, a medium present. I say apparently, because I am convinced that *somebody* is mediumistic, when people see or hear ghosts. The catalyst in a group may be the very person believing the least in the supernatural, but being endowed with certain characteristics that make him, or her, the natural intermediary between the Two Worlds!

When I investigate a "haunted house," I cannot sit around for days on end and hope for a fortunate moment when the discarnate entity has gathered up enough energy from the people in the house, or maybe passersby, or maybe me, to reveal himself. I am not usually asked to stay for a week. With me, it is tonight or never.

Therefore I like to make sure some sort of communication occurs at our first "sitting." To help matters along, I bring along a medium, preferably someone who does not earn his living in the capacity, although that is not absolutely necessary, provided he or she knows nothing about the location to be looked into.

Good mediums are rare. The talent, the innate inclination toward the psychic, is present in many of us, perhaps all. But the development to a stage where it can be of practical value is another matter. Good mediumship depends on rigorous training of the powers, discipline, and regular attempts at using it. Sporadic psychic application remains spotty. People who feel they have that *sixth sense* often ask me how to make it work for them. I usually advise them to put aside a few minutes every day, or every week, or even every two weeks, to "withdraw," and allow the power to come to the surface, in a moment of undisturbed silence. The important thing is to "sit" at precisely the same time, and to establish a certain rhythm in these sessions.

If the rhythm is interrupted, all the gains of previous weeks are lost; thus one must carefully choose a time and day when one is sure to be able to "sit" quietly. Sooner or later, mediumship will develop in one of its many forms.

Very few individuals attain the high development of a truly remarkable clairvoyant or trance medium, and there is of course a crying need in psychic research for such people. Thus a part of my attempts to look into ghosts and haunted houses has always been to replenish the supply of good mediums available to me for this work.

Whenever an individual, spurred on by one of my lectures or an article about me, has contacted me because he or she has psychic talents, I have followed up promptly in the hope of discovering, and perhaps encouraging, a new medium. So this is what I am to talk about now, and please forget your visions of mediums along Giancarlo Menotti lines. My mediums are all normal, everyday people who, by the very fact that they are mediumistic, need to be a bit more "normal" than you or I.

Mrs. Meyers, who appears in a large portion of the cases related in this book, is my first choice for a medium. Even Mrs. Meyers has her limitations, however, since she pursues a tiring career as a vocal coach and teacher. She devotes a great deal of time to psychic work, not only with me but with other researchers. Still, there are moments when the spirit—hers, that is—is only too willing, but the flesh isn't. By and large, however, she has scored very highly, and her mediumship is enhanced by a good working knowledge of the scientific aspects of her rare gifts.

Among the half dozen or more mediums I investigated or "sat" with in the course of the Grant Year (1960), and the following year, when assembling my book, I have found personalities as different as day and night. There was a kindly Negro woman, Nancy Hendricks, who told me on first meeting that a woman with the initial M., very close to me, wanted me to know that "life begins at forty." My mother's name was Martha, and I had turned forty the week before.

A lovely young woman by the name of Marina Brian

Agostini wrote to me as a consequence of a newspaper article about my work. I went to see her at her artistically appointed apartment on the Lower Eastside of New York, and was told that her first psychic experience had been at age seventeen, when she heard "a voice" telling her a cousin would soon die—and the cousin did. The night poet Maxwell Bodenheim was murdered, she dreamed of it, only to find the morning headlines confirming her dream!

While living at 307 Sixth Avenue, she noticed a "bearded beggar" leaning over her child's crib. Her husband, an artist, failed to see the stranger, but Marina insisted he had something to do with the house "being on fire." Shortly after, a fire was discovered next door. The apparition was a warning, evidently. Intrigued with the Unknown, Marina and three friends held a seance, during which she felt the presence of Eugene O'Neill, Junior, who had committed suicide in the apartment. She felt herself drawn to the bookcase and heard him say, "Look in my father's play for a message!" The message, the only line on the page indicated by the vision, was found to read, "There is no death"!

It is common for Mrs. Agostini to know the name of a caller before she picks up the telephone, or to see people she has dreamed of the night before, in the street the following day dressed exactly as they were in her dreams.

In 1959, Mrs. Agostini visited an allegedly haunted house in Center Moriches, Long Island, which belonged then to an advertising executive, but has since been turned into an inn. The owner had been plagued by psychic phenomena, including the opening of doors seemingly by their own volition, while securely locked. His wife once saw a person walk down the stairs, while she knew the maid was safely asleep in her quarters, and no one else about.

Unperturbed, Marina went up to the attic to look at the old house. To her amazement she found herself not alone. There, in front of a mirror, stood a blond girl, dressed in blue, combing her hair. All Marina could see was the girl's back; when she turned, however, Marina was frightened out of her wits by a face so full of unbridled hatred that it made her run down the stairs in stark terror!

Reporting her uncanny experience to her hosts, she was then told of the reputation of the house. A girl exactly like the one Marina had described was killed in this house the very night before her scheduled wedding!

One of her eerie experiences occurred when she was asked to read for the part of "Joan of Arc" in a play—but became uncontrollably agitated, and felt somehow that she was *present* when Joan died at the stake! Taken back to "an earlier life" hypnotically, she once spoke fluent ancient French—which she does not know in her ordinary state!

I arranged for a seance a few days later, to test her psychic abilities. The seance proved her to be a trance medium and highly susceptible. A personality calling himself "John" took her over, and told us that "I was killed . . . God help me." Later, Mrs. Agostini, who did not remember her trance utterances too well, thought the man was her uncle, whose death had been shrouded in mystery for some time.

I asked Marina whether she ever had a clairvoyant experience that prevented misfortune.

"Yes," she answered, "not long ago—in fact, last week. I planned to drive out to East Hampton in my uncle's car. The night before, as I was about to go to sleep, I had a sudden vision of a head-on collision involving his car, which I thought would happen the next day. I dismissed it from my mind, and didn't think of it again until the next day at about 5:30 when we were out in East Hampton, and about to start back to New York.

"We had just eaten in a restaurant out there, and were about to get back into the car, when my thirteen-year-old daughter Diane stated that she would rather sit *in the back* of the car with me than with my aunt and uncle in the front seat. I thought this *strange*, as she always prefers to sit in the front! Then I remembered my vision, and was disturbed by it again. As she got in, I wondered if some intuition made her choose the back seat, if we were to have an accident. I was happy she was back with me, but I was very concerned for my aunt and uncle in the front seat. I had of course not mentioned my vision to anyone.

"As we started to drive, I mentally put a protection (or a magic circle, as I refer to it) around the car, and felt a little better, but still uneasy. We had gone about twenty or thirty miles when a car coming quite fast from the opposite direction suddenly seemed to sway.

"I thought *this is the accident*, and had what seemed to be a blackout. The last thing I saw was the hub cap from the other car coming across the road and our hitting it. Then our car stopped, and my uncle got out to see the man in the other car, which also stopped, to reclaim his hub cap, but we had smashed it. I was trembling, and no one in the car could understand my overreaction, for it seemed a slight thing, hitting a hub cap. I felt very relieved, for I knew the accident had somehow been averted, with nothing more serious than a dented hub cap. I wondered if my 'magic circle' had saved us from the head-on collision that I had seen the night before in my vision!"

The day before our seance, Marina wrote me a note in which she described a series of dreamlike experiences she had had that night. Of particular interest to me was an apparition or spirit she described as "a young, slim, very beautiful, redheaded Scottish girl. I awoke with a terrible blow on the head, and I felt a 'presence' hovering over me. I told her to go away. She said she could take me to beautiful places; why did I want to get rid of her? This girl, I felt, was a seductress. She reminds me strongly of these lines from Keats' 'La Belle Dame Sans Merci':

'I met a lady in the meads,
Full beautiful—a fairy's child
Her hair was long, her foot was light,
and her eyes were wild.'"

It is true that we had sat down after the seance and talked about Scotland, for some reason. I had told Marina that I had always been drawn to things Scottish, and that I had constant and vague "impressions" of a girl somehow connected with me—perhaps in a previous life, if such can be proven. I did not go into any great details, however.

Now the girl Marina described so vividly to me hit me exactly as the "impression" I had had for several years. Moreover, in 1952 I wrote a song which went like this:

"One day, in the meadow, I met a fair Maid
I saw not her shadow, I saw not her shade
I bowed to the Maiden, and asked for her name,
And when she denied it, I asked whence she came.
She laughed and said, "Nowheres," and not one
    more word,
But when she had spoken, no echo was heard.
I swore that I loved her, she said I was sweet,
Then off she ran nimbly, though silent her feet.
Now if she be human, or if she be fay,
I'll love her, and truly, until my last day.
I'll be all her echo, her shadow, and sound—
To the Maid of the Meadow I've never since found!"

I had never heard of the Keats poem quoted to me by Marina. Coincidence? Psychic connections?

The late Clara Howard, sister of the justly famed West Coast medium, Sophia Williams, and undoubtedly possessed by similar gifts, once gave me a most complicated message that only I could properly place. It was her habit to tell a visitor on first contact all about his or her family.

Before I had time to collect my thoughts, she had rattled off things like, "A man in your mother's family died of a heart condition, and then there is also a Karl, and I get a name like Strauss, only it isn't quite that. You have two grandmothers, one you remember, one you don't, and your father was born just outside Vienna."

I was startled, for all this was correct. The name she had tried to "get" was Stransky, my mother's maiden name. I asked that my mother, whom she claimed to see, identify herself in some unmistakable way.

To my surprise, Clara Howard, who does not know the German language beyond a few broken words, came out with a sentence in perfect German: "*Kennst du das Land wo die Zitronen blühen?*" (Do you know the land where the lemons bloom?) I instantly recognized this as the title of a very lovely aria from the opera *Mignon*, and my mother's great favorite over the years.

Dorothy Jackson is a woman in her late forties working as a secretary. She is of good intelligence and in good health. Her records of paranormal experiences started in 1942; her father had passed on in 1941. She woke up one night, and, *while fully awake*, saw her father standing by her bedside. Thinking he had come for her, she said, "I'm not ready yet." However, it was not for her that her father had apparently come, but for her brother, who died soon after. Her father's apparition seemed exactly as he was in life, wearing a gray suit, but not quite as solid; she had the feeling that if she touched him, her hand would go through him, even though he looked solid enough. There was a luminous outline around his body.

Another favorite brother died in 1946. When in the

hospital, he sent for her. On her return from the hospital, she saw her father's materialized head on her shoulder. The brother died the same night.

Three times in past years she has "seen" neighbors or friends, usually only their heads; they died shortly thereafter. She has these visions only when she is very relaxed, in the evenings.

Very often she dreams of visiting strange places and seeing people both known and unknown to her; when she awakens in the morning, she finds her feet *physically tired as if from long walking about*!

Two years ago, she had a dream in which she saw four rooms. In each of the first three rooms was one of the three men in her life up to that time; in the fourth room she saw a man she had been corresponding with, and with whom she was then on excellent terms. Nevertheless she knew in that dream that their relationship was to end. Six months later it did.

One of the more gifted mediums I have met is Betty Ritter, whose particular phase is a combination of clairvoyance and trance. I have sat with her many times, and never gone home empty-handed. I remember meeting her first in 1954, at an experimental session conducted at the quarters of the Association for Research and Enlightenment. At that time, she came toward me at the close of the session and asked, rather abruptly—"Are you Hans Holzer?"

When I nodded, she said, in a puzzled voice, "There is a man here who claims to be an uncle of yours."

I have many uncles. I asked for some details so I could recognize the caller.

Betty closed her eyes for a moment. "His initials are O. S.," she then said quietly, "and he's got a blond wife. Her name is Alice!"

I was taken aback. My late uncle Otto Stransky, the composer, had died under tragic circumstances in a streetcar accident. His wife's name was indeed Alice, but— so many years having gone by—she was no longer a blonde. Her hair was by now a mature gray. Still, to the memory of my uncle, she would always be a blonde!

Six years went by until I had occasion to meet Betty Ritter again. She described to me a girl with the name of Lisa. Now the curious thing is that this friend, who died under tragic circumstances, too, had not been named Lisa but Joan. But with her close friends, she preferred to be called Lisa instead!

Florence, the psychometrist, has on occasion shown how good a clairvoyant she can be. I remember one night in July 1960, when a large number of people were present at the home of Dr. S. Kahn, the psychiatrist, of Harmon, New York. Florence looked around, not recognizing any of the faces. "There's been a controversy about a grave," she said with determination. Florence always seems sure of her facts.

"About seven or eight years ago, a five-year-old child was paralyzed in the legs and passed on. Someone said

'I can't go on much longer.' I think the mother is in this room."

With this, Florence looked into the semidarkened room, waiting. She didn't have to wait long. A Mrs. Harry Davies rose and acknowledged that her six-year-old boy had been run over by a car, and that the sentence Florence had quoted was spoken exactly seven years ago!

Then the medium turned to her host and said, "There's a man named Felder, or something like it, here; he says he was a patient in your hospital."

Dr. Kahn nodded gravely. "His name was Feldman," he replied, "and he died recently."

Carolyn Chapman is often considered the dean of mediums. This wonderfully spunky Southern lady received me one day in November 1960, after a lapse of more than six years. We talked about the family contacts that might be received by her clairvoyantly, and immediately she spoke of my grandmother, Anna; my mother, Martha; my cousins, Albert and Fred; my Uncle, Julius; and Karl. That's five names out of five. Naturally, I had not mentioned any names to her! Interesting, too, was Marion Klein, a diminutive psychic who likes to help people find the spiritual way. Once, during a seance held at the Burr Galleries in mid-Manhattan, she turned to a man she was seeing for the first time in her life, and inquired—"Are you a stone mason?"

Luigi Bartolomo is a sculptor.

"I seem to be talking to a Mr. and Mrs. Martino," Marion Klein continued. "Do you know them?"

"Yes," the sculptor nodded, "I do. They've been dead for some time."

Not all seance experiences are of a grim nature. Some, in fact, do not lack a sense of humor. Such was the case when Ethel Johnson-Meyers and I descended upon the West 56th Street premises of a fancy restaurant called the Da Vinci. It appeared that a certain advertising executive, who had been a frequent guest at the place, and who was given to much drinking, had recently killed himself in his Eastside apartment. A close friend, Juleen Compton, actually "saw" his ghost there, but that is not unusual, from my point of view. Lots of apartments are haunted.

However, the ghost of the ad man was not content to roam his former home; he decided to descend as well upon his home-away-from-home, where he had spent many a long night in the company of a good drink, or a series of them.

Before long, the proprietors found empty Martini glasses on the bar, when they *knew* none had been there at closing time. Advertising slogans were found scribbled on the walls, but no one had seen the scribbler.

When Mrs. Meyers had seated herself behind the long table that runs the entire length of the place, the ghost took hold of her speech mechanism and immediately demanded a drink! In fact, he behaved in such an alcoholic manner that Mrs. Meyer, a very proper lady, would have been horrified to see her face and actions, under the influence of the discarnate gentleman! Pressed by me about his last day on earth, he finally mumbled that he had spent it with Allan. On later investigation, Allan was found to be his closest friend—a fact Mrs. Meyers could not possibly have known!

A ghost hunter without mediums is like an angler without fish—but the important thing is to be always on the alert against deception, both willful and innocent. Nothing is as dangerous as self-delusion, and I have always allowed more than a generous margin for error in psychic evidence. Still, with all these allowances, the fact remains—there are a number of medically healthy individuals who can make contact with what Dr. J. Rhine calls "The World of the Mind."

No chapter on mediums would be complete without an account of psychic photography. There are those researchers who firmly believe it is all fraud. Then there are those who think every psychic photography medium is genuine. Neither is the case, in my opinion. But twice I have had firsthand proof, from medium John Myers, who produced exact likenesses of my late aunt and mother—without of course having access to my family album or any other source of supply.

During September 1961, John Myers demonstrated his gift for psychic photography on the Mike Wallace television program called "PM–EAST." Millions of viewers saw Myers, heard him discuss his past achievements, and then saw him show some of the outstanding psychic photography and skotographs taken by Myers over the years.

Among the remarkable pictures shown was the one taken by Myers at the funeral of Lady Caillard, where he did not even get near the plates used, which were placed on the coffin by a news photographer at the funeral. This picture had the "extras" of Lord Caillard and Lady Caillard, as well as Arthur Conan Doyle on them. On this same television program, John Myers and I also showed the psychic photograph of Myers' mother, the first such picture received through his mediumship, and several others taken in his presence by experimenters in England, to demonstrate the differences between normal and psychic photographs.

After that, Mike Wallace produced an uncut package of photographic paper from his pocket, and held it up to the camera, asserting for all to hear that he himself had purchased this ordinary photographic paper that afternoon, and had kept the sealed and signed package in his possession continuously. And now, on camera, he would open it on the instructions of John Myers. Before us we had three trays, filled with developing fluid, hypo, and water. Overhead, only a single 60-watt yellow bulb illuminated the somewhat eerie scene as Mike Wallace, flanked on either side by John Myers and myself, proceeded to open the package of sensitive papers. Then he plunged them one by one into the liquid.

At first, nothing happened, and the silence hung heavy as millions of people all over the United States watched in awe. Wallace started to joke about unwillingness of spirits to show themselves on his show. But then, suddenly, forms began to appear on the papers.

Excitement mounted. At first, only amorphous shapes

came up; but one or two rapidly took on the appearance of heads, and there was a figure and an arm beginning to take form. But, alas—air time being precious, we could no longer stay on camera; the program had to continue. Although Wallace admitted publicly that these "shapes" shouldn't be there to begin with, and that they did indeed look somewhat like faces, we could not wait for them to clearly develop, as clearly as previous Myers psychic photographs have done.

Nevertheless, it was a coup of the first order—psychic photography on live television for the first time, anywhere.

When we went off the air, we scooped up the psychic photographs, and Myers put them into the envelope they had come in. Not thinking anything further about the matter—for psychic photographs are "old hat" to Myers by now—he took them home with him: there he decided to wash them, since there had been insufficient time on the air to clean them of the hypo. When he withdrew the pictures from the water, he discovered that several heads had come up much clearer, and others had been added, somehow, during the journey from the studio to his home.

Casually, John Myers showed me the results. To my amazement, I found that one of the psychic pictures was that of my own mother, who had passed in 1954. I located a very similar photograph of her in my family album, taken when she was still in good health, about fifteen years before!

THE GHOSTLY
LOVER

Perhaps the most fantastic case of recent vintage is a case involving Betty Ritter and the well-known psychoanalyst Dr. Nandor Fodor. Dr. Fodor had been treating a certain Edith Berger, in Long Island, for what seemed at first disturbing symptoms of split personality. But Dr. Fodor is a trained parapsychologist as well, and he did not fail to recognize the case for what it was, possession!

He suggested that the Bergers call in a good medium, and recommended Betty Ritter.

Half in tears, Edith Berger's mother told Betty on the telephone how a possessive spirit personality had been annoying her and her daughter for the past four months. It seemed that Edith, the daughter, had a gentleman friend, a medical doctor, who had died in the tropics not long before.

The very day after his death, the young woman found that her erstwhile suitor had attached himself to her, and was forcing himself on her—physically! The attacks were so violent, the mother said, that she had to sleep in the same bed with her daughter for protection, but to no avail. The mother also *felt* the physical contact experienced by her daughter!

Betty concentrated her psychic powers immediately on what can only be called a form of exorcism. Although there was some relief, the ghostly boy friend was still around.

To Betty's horror, she woke up that same night to find the restless one standing before her bed, stark naked, in a menacing mood. Betty's contacts on "the other side," however, protected her and took the erring one away.

Telling Edith Berger of her experience the next day, she accurately described the visitor. Her efforts seemed to weaken the attacks somewhat, and several days later she saw him again, this time, however, fully clothed! He wore riding boots and carried a whip. The Bergers confirmed that the man had been a lover of horses. On April 20th, 1961, Betty Ritter telephoned the Bergers to find out how things were going. The moment Edith answered the telephone, the ghost started to pull her hair in a most painful fashion, as if to prove he was still very much in evidence!

But the violent mind of the young doctor would not accept the separation from his physical body and its pleasures. The haunting continued; thus Betty Ritter asked me to accompany her to the Berger home for another go at the case.

The Bergers turned out to be very level-headed middle-class people, and completely ignorant of anything psychic. Edith seemed to be a highly nervous, but quite "normal" human being. Almost immediately, the entity got hold of the medium and yelled through her—"I shall not be pulled away from you. I won't go."

I learned that the father had at first been highly skeptical of all this, but his daughter's behavior changed so much, and became so different from her previous character, that he had to admit to himself that something uncanny was happening in his house. Edith, who had wanted to be a singer, and was far from tidy, suddenly became the very model of tidyness, started to clean up things, and behaved like a nurse—the profession her late boy friend had wanted her to follow. At times, she assumed his ailments and "passing symptoms." At times, she would suffer from genuine malaria—just as he had done. Since Edith was mediumistic, it was easy for the dead doctor to have his will. The message he wanted her to deliver most was to tell his mother that he was "still alive." But how could she do that, and not reveal her agony?

One afternoon, while she was praying for him, she felt a clutching sensation on her arm. Later on, in bed, she clearly heard his voice, saying—"It is me, Don!" From that day on, he stayed with her constantly. On one particular amorous occasion, *her mother clearly discerned a man's outline in the empty bed*. She quickly grabbed a fly swatter and chased the earthbound spirit out of her daughter's bed!

Once, when she was about to put on her coat to go out,

the coat, apparently of its own volition, came toward her—as if someone were holding it for her to slip on!

Whenever she was with other men, he kissed her, and she would hear his angry voice.

But this time the seance cracked his selfish shell. "I haven't been able to finish what I started," he sobbed, referring to his important medical experiments. He then asked forgiveness, and that he be allowed to come back to be with Edith now and then.

After we left—Dr. Fodor had come along, too—we all expressed hope that the Bergers would live in peace. But a few weeks later, Edith telephoned me in great excitement. The doctor had returned once more.

I then explained to her that she had to sacrifice—rid herself of her own *desire* to have this man around, unconscious though it may be—and in closing the door on this chapter of her life, make it impossible for the earthbound one to take control of her psychic energies. I have heard nothing further.

THE CASE OF THE MURDERED FINANCIER

I remember the night we went to visit the house where financier Serge Rubinstein was killed. It was a year after his death but only I, among the group, had knowledge of the exact date of the anniversary. John Latouche, my much-too-soon departed friend, and I picked up Mrs. Meyers at her Westside home and rode in a taxi to Fifth Avenue and 60th Street. As a precaution, so as not to give away the address which we were headed for, we left the taxi two blocks south of the Rubinstein residence.

Our minds were careful blanks, and the conversation was about music. But we didn't fool our medium. "What's the pianist doing here?" she demanded to know. What pianist, I countered. "Rubinstein," said she. For to our medium, a professional singing teacher, that name could only stand for the great pianist. It showed that our medium was, so to speak, on-the-beam, and already entering into the "vibration," or electrically charged atmosphere of the haunting.

Latouche and I looked at each other in amazement. Mrs. Meyers was puzzled by our sudden excitement. Without further delay, we rang the bell at the stone mansion, hoping the door would open quickly so that we would not be exposed to curiosity-seekers who were then still hanging around the house where one of the most publicized murders had taken place just a year before, to the hour.

It was now near midnight, and my intention had been to try and make contact with the spirit of the departed. I assumed, from the manner in which he died, that Serge Rubinstein might still be around his house, and I had gotten his mother's permission to attempt the contact.

The seconds on the doorstep seemed like hours, as Mrs. Meyers questioned me about the nature of tonight's "case." I asked her to be patient, but when the butler came and finally opened the heavy gate, Mrs. Meyers suddenly realized where we were. "It isn't the pianist, then!" she mumbled, somewhat dazed. "It's the *other* Rubinstein!" With these words we entered the forbidding-looking building for an evening of horror and ominous tension.

Eight years after the murder, it is still officially unsolved, and as much an enigma to the world as it was on that cold winter night, in 1955, when the newspaper headlines screamed of "bad boy" financier Serge Rubinstein's untimely demise. That night, after business conferences and a night on the town with a brunette, Rubinstein had some unexpected visitors. Even the District Attorney couldn't name them for sure, but there were suspects galore, and the investigation never ran out of possibilities.

Evidently Serge had a falling-out with the brunette, Estelle Gardner, and decided the evening was still young, so he felt like continuing it with a change of cast. Another girl, Pat Wray, later testified that Rubinstein telephoned her to join him, after he had gotten rid of Estelle, *and that she refused.*

The following morning, the butler, William Morter, found Rubinstein dead in his third-floor bedroom. He was wearing pajamas, and evidently the victim of some form of torture—for his arms and feet were tied, and his mouth and throat thickly covered by adhesive tape. The medical examiner dryly ruled death caused by strangulation.

The police found themselves with a first-rate puzzle on their hands. Lots of people wanted to kill Rubinstein, lots of people had said so publicly without meaning it—but who actually did? The financier's reputation was not the best, although it must be said that he did no more nor less than many others; but his manipulations were neither elegant nor quiet, and consequently, the glaring light of publicity and exposure created a public image of a monster that did not really fit the Napoleonic-looking young man from Paris.

Rubinstein was a possessive and jealous man. A tiny microphone was placed by him in the apartment of Pat Wray, sending sound into a tape recorder hidden in a car parked outside the building. Thus, Rubinstein was able to monitor her every word!

Obviously, his dealings were worldwide, and there were some 2,000 names in his private files.

The usual sensational news accounts had been seen in the press the week prior to our seance, but none of them contained anything new or definite. Mrs. Meyers' knowledge of the case was as specific as that of any ordinary newspaper reader.

We were received by Serge's seventy-nine-year-old mother, Stella Rubinstein; her sister, Eugenia Forrester; the Rubinstein attorney, Ennis; a girl secretary; a guard named Walter, and a newspaper reporter from a White Russian paper, Jack Zwieback. After a few moments of polite talk downstairs—that is, on the second floor where the library of the sumptuous mansion was located—I suggested we go to the location of the crime itself.

We all rose, when Mrs. Meyers suddenly stopped in her tracks. "I feel someone's grip on my arm," she commented.

We went upstairs without further incidents. The bedroom of the slain financier was a medium-size room in the rear of the house, connected with the front sitting room through a large bathroom. We formed a circle around the bed, occupying the center of the room. The light was subdued, but the room was far from dark. It was just twenty minutes after nine. Mrs. Meyers insisted on sitting in a chair close to the bed, and remarked that she "was directed there."

Gradually her body relaxed, her eyes closed, and the heavy, rhythmic breathing of onsetting trance was heard in the silence of the room, heavily tensed with fear and apprehension of what was to come.

Several times, the medium placed her arm before her face, as if warding off attacks; symptoms of choking distorted her face and a struggle seemed to take place before our eyes!

Within a few minutes, this was over, and a new strange voice came from the lips of the medium. "I can speak . . . over there, they're coming!" The arm pointed toward the bathroom.

I asked who "they" were.

"They're no friends . . . Joe, Stan . . . cheap girl . . . in the door, they—" The hand went to the throat, indicating choking.

Then, suddenly, the person in command of the medium added: "The woman should be left out. There was a calendar with serial numbers . . . box numbers, but they can't get it! Freddie was here, too!"

"What was in the box?"

"Fourteen letters. Nothing for the public."

"Give me more information."

"Baby-Face . . . I don't want to talk too much . . . they'll pin it on Joe."

"How many were there?"

"Joe, Stan, and Freddie . . . stooges. Her bosses' stooges! London . . . let me go, let me go . . . I'm too frantic here . . . not up here . . . I'll come again."

With a jolt, the medium awoke from her trance. Perspiration stood on her forehead, although the room was cold. Not a word was said by the people in the room. Mrs. Meyers leaned back and thought for a moment.

"I feel a small, stocky man here, perverted minds, and there is fighting all over the room. He is being surprised by the bathroom door. They were hiding in the next room, came through this window and fire escape."

We descended again to the library, where we had originally assembled. The conversation continued quietly, when suddenly Mrs. Meyers found herself rapidly slipping into trance again.

"Three men, one wiry and tall, one short and very stocky, and one tall and stout—the shorter one is in charge. Then there is Baby-Face . . . she has a Mona Lisa–like face. Stan is protected. I had the goods on them. . . . Mama's right, it's getting hot. . . ."

"Give us the name!" I almost shouted. Tension gripped us all.

The medium struggled with an unfamiliar sound. "Kapoich . . . ?" Then she added, "The girl here . . . poker face."

"But what is her name?"

"Ha ha . . . tyrant."

When Mrs. Meyers came out of her trance, I questioned Rubinstein's mother about the seance. She readily agreed that the voice had indeed sounded much like her late son's. Moreover, there was that girl—named in the investigation— who had a "baby face." She never showed emotion, and was, in fact, poker-faced all the time. Her name?

"My son often called her his tyrant," the mother said, visibly shaken. "What about the other names?"

"My son used a hired limousine frequently. The chauffeur was a stocky man, and his name was Joe or Joey. Stan? I have heard that name many times in business conversations." One of the men involved in the investigation was named Kubitschek. Had the deceased tried to pronounce that name?

A wallet once belonging to Serge had been handed to Mrs. Meyers a few minutes before, to help her maintain contact with the deceased. Suddenly, without warning, the wallet literally *flew out of her hands* and hit the high ceiling of the library with tremendous impact.

Mrs. Meyers' voice again sounded strange, as the late financier spoke through her in anger. "Do you know how much it costs to sell a man down the river?"

Nobody cared to answer. We had all had quite enough for one evening!

We all left in different directions, and I sent a duplicate of the seance transcript to the police, something I have done with every subsequent seance as well. Mrs. Meyers and I were never the only ones to know what transpired in trance. The police knew, too, and if they did not choose to arrest anyone, that was their business.

We were sure our seance had not attracted attention, and Mrs. Rubinstein herself, and her people, certainly would not spread the word of the unusual goings-on in the Fifth Avenue mansion on the anniversary of the murder.

But on February 1, Cholly Knickerbocker headlined—
"Serge's Mother Holds A Seance"!

Not entirely accurate in his details—his source turned
out to be one of the guards—Mr. Cassini, nevertheless,
came to the point in stating: "To the awe of all present, no
less than four people were named by the medium. If this
doesn't give the killers the chills, it certainly does us."

We thought we had done our bit toward the solution of
this baffling murder, and were quite prepared to forget the
excitement of that evening. Unfortunately, the wraith of
Rubinstein did not let it rest at that.

During a routine seance then held at my house on West
70th Street, he took over the medium's personality, and
elaborated on his statements. He talked of his offices in
London and Paris, his staff, and his enemies. One of his
lawyers, Rubinstein averred, knew more than he *dared*
disclose!

I called Mrs. Rubinstein and arranged for another, less
public sitting at the Fifth Avenue house. This time only the
four of us, the two elderly ladies, Mrs. Meyers and I, were
present. Rubinstein's voice was again recognized by his
mother.

"It was at 2:45 on the nose. 2:45!" he said, speaking of
the time of his death. "Pa took my hand, it wasn't so bad.
I want to tell the little angel woman here, I don't always
listen like a son should—she told me always, 'You go too far,
don't take chances!'"

Then his voice grew shrill with anger. "Justice will be
done. I have paid for that."

I asked, what did this fellow Joey, whom he mentioned the first time, do for a living?

"Limousines. He knew how to come. He brought them here, they were not invited."

He then added something about Houston, Texas, and insisted that a man from that city was involved. He was sure "the girl" would eventually talk and break the case.

There were a number of other sittings, at my house, where the late Serge put his appearance into evidence. Gradually, his hatred and thirst for revenge gave way to a calmer acceptance of his untimely death. He kept us informed of "poker face's moves"—whenever the girl moved, Serge was there to tell us. Sometimes his language was rough, sometimes he held back.

"They'll get Mona Lisa," he assured me on March 30th, 1956. I faithfully turned the records of our seances over to the police. They always acknowledged them, but were not eager to talk about this help from so odd a source as a psychical researcher!

Rubinstein kept talking about a Crown Street Headquarters in London, but we never were able to locate this address. At one time, he practically insisted on taking his medium with him into the street, to look for his murderers! It took strength and persuasion for me to calm the restless one, for I did not want Mrs. Meyers to leave the safety of the big armchair by the fireplace, which she usually occupied at our seances.

"Stan is on this side now," he commented on April 13th.

I could never fathom whether Stan was his friend or his

enemy, or perhaps both at various times. Financier Stanley died a short time after our initial seance at the Fifth Avenue mansion.

Safe deposit boxes were mentioned, and numbers given, but somehow Mrs. Rubinstein never managed to find them.

On April 26th, we held another sitting at my house. This time the spirit of the slain financier was particularly restless.

"Vorovsky," he mumbled, "yellow cab, he was paid good for helping her get away from the house. Doug paid him, he's a friend of Charley's. Tell mother to hire a private detective."

I tried to calm him. He flared up at me. "Who're you talking to? The Pope?"

The next day, I checked these names with his mother. Mrs. Rubinstein also assured me that the expression "who do you think I am—the Pope?" was one of his favorite phrases in life!

"Take your nose down to Texas and you'll find a long line to London and Paris," he advised us on May 10th.

Meanwhile, Mrs. Rubinstein increased the reward for the capture of the murderer to $50,000. Still, no one was arrested, and the people the police had originally questioned had all been let go. Strangely enough, the estate was much smaller than at first anticipated. Was much money still in hiding, perhaps in some unnamed safe deposit box? We'll never know. Rubinstein's mother has gone on to join him on the Other Side of the Veil, too.

My last contact with the case was in November of 1961,

when columnist Hy Gardner asked me to appear on his television program. We talked about the Rubinstein seances, and he showed once more the eerie bit of film he called "a collector's item"—the only existing television interview with Rubinstein, made shortly before his death in 1955.

The inquisitive reporter's questions are finally parried by the wily Rubinstein with an impatient—"Why, that's like asking a man about his own death!"

Could it be that Serge Rubinstein, in addition to all his other "talents," also had the gift of prophecy?

THE ROCKLAND
COUNTY GHOST*

I n November 1951 the writer heard for the first time of the haunted house belonging to the late Danton Walker, the well-known newspaper man.

Over a dinner table in a Manhattan restaurant, the strange goings-on in the Rockland County house were discussed with me for the first time, although they had been observed over the ten years preceding our meeting. The manifestations had come to a point where they had forced Mr. Walker to leave his house to the ghost and build himself a studio on the other end of his estate, where he was able to live unmolested.

A meeting with Mrs. Garrett was soon arranged, but due to her indisposition, it had to be postponed. Despite

---

* Courtesy of *Tomorrow*, Vol. I, No. 3.

her illness, Mrs. Garrett, in a kind of "traveling clairvoy-ance," did obtain a clairvoyant impression of the entity. His name was "Andreas," and she felt him to be rather attached to the present owner of the house. These findings Mrs. Garrett communicated to Mr. Walker, but nothing further was done on the case until the fall of 1952. A "rescue circle" operation was finally organized on November 22, 1952, and successfully concluded the case, putting the disturbed soul to rest and allowing Mr. Walker to return to the main house without further fear of manifestations.

Before noting the strange phenomena that have been observed in the house, it will be necessary to describe this house a bit, as the nature of the building itself has a great deal to do with the subsequent occurrences.

Mr. Walker's house is a fine example of colonial archi-tecture, of the kind that was built in the country during the second half of the eighteenth century. Although Walker was sure only of the first deed to the property, dated 1813 and naming the Abrams family, of pre-Revolutionary origin in the country, the house itself is unquestionably much older.

When Mr. Walker bought the house in the spring of 1942, it was in the dismal state of disrepair typical of some dwellings in the surrounding Ramapo Mountains. It took the new owner several years and a great deal of money to rebuild the house to its former state and to refurbish it with the furniture, pewter, and other implements of the period. I am mentioning this point because in its present state the house is a completely livable and authentic colonial building of the kind that would be an entirely familiar and a welcome sight to a man living toward the end of the eighteenth century, were he to set foot into it today.

The house stands on a hill which was once part of a farm. During the War for Independence, this location was the headquarters of a colonial army. In fact, "Mad" Anthony Wayne's own headquarters stood near this site, and the Battle of Stony Point (1779) was fought a few miles away. Most likely, the building restored by Mr. Walker was then in use as a fortified roadhouse, used both for storage of arms, ammunitions, and food supplies, and for the temporary lodging of prisoners.

After the house passed from the hands of the Abrams family in the earlier part of the last century, a banker named Dixon restored the farm and the hill, but paid scant attention to the house itself. By and by, the house gave in to the ravages of time and weather. A succession of mountain people made it their living quarters around the turn of the century, but did nothing to improve its sad state of disrepair. When Mr. Walker took over, only the kitchen and a small adjoining room were in use; the rest of the house was filled with discarded furniture and other objects. The upstairs was divided into three tiny rooms and a small attic, which disgorged bonnets, hoop skirts, and crudely carved wooden shoe molds and toys, dating from about the Civil War period.

While the house was being reconstructed, Mr. Walker was obliged to spend nights at a nearby inn, but would frequently take naps during the day on an army cot upstairs.

On these occasions he received distinct impressions of "a Revolutionary soldier" being in the room.

Mr. Walker's moving in, in the spring of 1942, touched off the usual country gossip, some of which later reached his ears. *It seemed that the house was haunted.* One woman who had lived in the place told of an "old man" who frightened the children, mysterious knocks at the front door, and other mysterious happenings. But none of these reports could be followed up. For all practical purposes, we may say that the phenomena started with the arrival of Mr. Walker.

Though Mr. Walker was acutely sensitive to the atmosphere of the place from the time he took over, it was not until 1944 that the manifestations resulted in both visible and audible phenomena. That year, during an afternoon when he was resting in the front room downstairs, he was roused by a violent summons to the front door, which has a heavy iron knocker. Irritated by the intrusion when no guest was expected, he called "Come in!" then went to the front door and found no one there.

About this time, Mr. Walker's butler, Johnny, remarked to his employer that the house was a nice place to stay in "if they would let you alone." Questioning revealed that Johnny, spending the night in the house alone, had gone downstairs three times during the night to answer knocks at the front door. An Italian workman named Pietro, who did some repairs on the house, reported sounds of someone walking up the stairs in midafternoon "with heavy boots on," at a time when there definitely was no one else in the place. Two occasional guests of the owner also were disturbed, while reading in the living room, by the sound of heavy footsteps overhead.

In 1950 Mr. Walker and his secretary were eating dinner in the kitchen, which is quite close to the front door. There was a sharp rap at the door. The secretary opened it and found nobody there. In the summer of 1952, when there were guests downstairs but no one upstairs, sounds of heavy thumping were heard from upstairs, *as if someone had taken a bad fall.*

Though Mr. Walker, his butler, and his guests never saw or fancied they saw any ghostly figures, the manifestations did not restrict themselves to audible phenomena. Unexplainable dents in pewter pieces occurred from time to time. A piece of glass in a door pane, the same front door of the house, was cracked but remained solidly in place for some years. One day it was missing and could not be located in the hall indoors, nor outside on the porch. A week later this four-by-four piece of glass was accidentally found resting on a plate rail eight feet above the kitchen floor. How it got there is as much of a mystery now as it was then.

On one occasion, when Johnny was cleaning the stairs to the bedroom, a picture that had hung at the top of the stairs for at least two years tumbled down, almost striking him. A woman guest who had spent the night on a daybed in the living room, while making up the bed next morning, was almost struck by a heavy pewter pitcher which fell ("almost as if thrown at her") from a bookshelf hanging behind the bed. There were no unusual vibrations of the house to account for these things.

On the white kitchen wall there are heavy semicircular black marks where a pewter salt box, used for holding keys, had been violently swung back and forth. A large pewter pitcher, which came into the house in perfect condition, now bears five heavy imprints, four on one side, one on the other. A West Pointer with unusually large hands fitted his own four fingers and thumb into the dents!

Other phenomena include the gripping chills felt from time to time by Mr. Walker and his more sensitive guests. These chills, not to be confused with drafts, were felt in all parts of the house by Mr. Walker when alone. They took the form of a sudden paralyzing cold, as distinct as a cramp. Such a chill once seized him when he had been ill and gone to bed early. Exasperated by the phenomenon, he unthinkingly called out aloud, "Oh, for God's sake, let me alone!" The chill abruptly stopped.

But perhaps the most astounding incident took place in November 1952, only a few days before the rescue circle met at the house.

Two of Mr. Walker's friends, down-to-earth men with no belief in the so-called supernatural, were weekend guests. Though Walker suggested that they both spend the night in the commodious studio about three hundred feet from the main house, one of them insisted on staying upstairs in the "haunted" room. Walker persuaded him to leave the lights on.

An hour later, the pajama-clad man came rushing down to the studio, demanding that Mr. Walker put an end "to his pranks." The light beside his bed was blinking on and off. All *other lights* in the house were burning steadily!

Assured that this might be caused by erratic power supply and that no one was playing practical jokes, the guest returned to the main house. But an hour or so later, he came back to the studio and spent the rest of the night there. In the morning he somewhat sheepishly told that he had been awakened from a sound sleep by the sensation of someone slapping him violently in the face. Sitting bolt upright in bed, he noticed that the shirt he had hung on the back of a rocking chair was being agitated by the "breeze." Though admitting that this much might have been pure imagination, he also seemed to notice the chair gently rocking. Since all upstairs windows were closed, there definitely was no "breeze."

"The sensation described by my guest," Mr. Walker remarked, "reminded me of a quotation from one of Edith Wharton's ghost stories. Here is the exact quote:

"'Medford sat up in bed with a jerk which resembles no other. Someone was in his room. The fact reached him not by sight or sound . . . but by a peculiar faint disturbance of the invisible currents that enclose us.'

"Many people in real life have experienced this sensation. I myself had not spent a night alone in the main house in four years. It got so that I just couldn't take it. In fact, I built the studio specifically to get away from staying there. When people have kidded me about my 'haunted house,' my reply is, would I have spent so much time and money restoring the house, and then built another house to spend the night in, if there had not been some valid reason?"

On many previous occasions, Mr. Walker had remarked that he had a feeling that someone was trying "desperately" to get into the house, as if for refuge. The children of an earlier tenant had mentioned some agitation "by the lilac bush" at the corner of the house. The original crude walk from the road to the house, made of flat native stones, passed this lilac bush and went to the well, which, according to local legend, was used by soldiers in Revolutionary times.

"When I first took over the place," Mr. Walker observed, "I used to look out of the kitchen window twenty times a day to see who was at the well. Since the old walk has been replaced by a stone walk and driveway, no one could now come into the place without being visible for at least sixty-five feet. Following the reconstruction, the stone wall blocking the road was torn down several times at the exact spot where the original walk reached the road."

In all the disturbances which led to the efforts of the rescue circle, I detected one common denominator. Someone was attempting to get into the house, and to call attention to something. Playing pranks, puzzling people, or even frightening them, were not part of the "ghost's" purpose; they were merely his desperate devices for getting attention, attention for something he very much wanted to say.

On a bleak and foreboding day in November 1952, the little group comprising the rescue circle drove out into the country for the sitting. They were accompanied by

Dr. L., a prominent Park Avenue psychiatrist and psycho-analyst, and of course by Mr. Walker, the owner of the property.

The investigation was sponsored by Parapsychology Foundation, Inc., of New York City. Participants included Mrs. Eileen J. Garrett; Dr. L., whose work in psychiatry and analysis is well known; Miss Lenore Davidson, assistant to Mrs. Garrett, who was responsible for most of the notes taken; Dr. Michel Pobers, then Secretary General of the Parapsychology Foundation; and myself.

The trip to the Rockland Country home of Mr. Walker took a little over an hour. The house stands atop a wide hill, not within easy earshot of the next inhabited house, but not too far from his own "cabin" and two other small houses belonging to Mr. Walker's estate. The main house, small and compact, represents a perfect restoration of Colonial American architecture.

A plaque in the ground at the entrance gate calls atten-tion to the historical fact that General Wayne's headquarters at the time of the Battle of Stony Point, 1779, occupied the very same site. Mr. Walker's house was possibly part of the fortification system protecting the hill, and no doubt served as a stronghold in the war of 1779 and in earlier wars and campaigns fought around this part of the country. One feels the history of many generations clinging to the place.

We took our place in the upstairs bedroom, grouping ourselves so as to form an imperfect circle around Mrs. Garrett, who sat in a heavy, solid wooden chair with her back to the wall and her face toward us.

The time was 2:45 P.M. and the room was fully lit by ample daylight coming in through the windows.

After a moment, Mrs. Garrett placed herself in full trance by means of autohypnosis. Quite suddenly her own personality vanished, and the medium sank back into her chair completely lifeless, very much like an unused garment discarded for the time being by its owner. But not for long. A few seconds later, another personality "got into" the medium's body, precisely the way one dons a shirt or coat. It was Uvani, one of Mrs. Garrett's two spirit guides who act as her control personalities in all of her experiments. Uvani, in his own lifetime, was an East Indian of considerable knowledge and dignity, and as such he now appeared before us.

As "he" sat up—I shall refer to the distinct personalities now using the "instrument" (the medium's body) as "he" or "him"—it was obvious that we had before us a gentleman from India. Facial expression, eyes, color of skin, movements, the folded arms, and the finger movements that accompanied many of his words were all those of a native of India. As Uvani addressed us, he spoke in perfect English, except for a faltering word now and then or an occasional failure of idiom, but his accent was typical.

At this point, the tape recorder faithfully took down every word spoken. The transcript given here is believed to be complete, and is certainly so where we deal with Uvani, who spoke clearly and slowly. In the case of the ghost, much of the speech was garbled because of the ghost's unfortunate condition; some of the phrases were repeated several times, and a few words were so badly uttered that they could not be made out by any of us. In order to present only verifiable evidence, I have eliminated all such words and report here nothing which was not completely understandable and clear. But at least seventy percent of the words uttered by the ghost, and of course all of the words of Uvani, are on record. The tape recording is supplemented by Miss Davidson's exacting transcript, and in the final moments her notes replace it entirely.

Uvani: It is I, Uvani. I give you greetings, friends. Peace be with you, and in your lives, and in this house!

Dr. L.: And our greetings to you, Uvani. We welcome you.

Uvani: I am very happy to speak with you, my good friend. (Bows to Dr. L.) You are out of your native element.

Dr. L.: Very much so. We have not spoken in this environment at all before. . . .

Uvani: What is it that you would have of me today, please?

Dr. L.: We are met here as friends of Mr. Walker, whose house this is, to investigate strange occurrences which have taken place in this house from time to time, which lead us to feel that they partake of the nature of this field of interest of ours.

We would be guided by you, Uvani, as to the
method of approach which we should use this
afternoon. Our good friend and instrument (Mrs.
Garrett) has the feeling that there was a personality
connected with this house whose influence is still
to be felt here.

Uvani: Yes, I would think so. I am confronted myself
with a rather restless personality. In fact, a very
strange personality, and one that might appear to
be in his own life perhaps not quite of the right
mind—I think you would call it.

I have a great sense of agitation. I would like to
tell you about this personality, and at the same time
draw your attention to the remarkable—what you
might call—atmospherics that he is able to bring
into our environment. You, who are my friend and
have worked with me very much, know that when I
am in control, we are very calm—yes? Yet it is as
much as I can do to maintain the control, as you
see—for such is the atmosphere produced by this
personality, that you will note my own difficulty to
restrain and constrain the instrument. (The
medium's hand shakes in rapid palsy. Uvani's voice
trembles.) This one, in spite of me, by virtue of his
being with us brings into the process of our field of
work a classical palsy. Do you see this?

Dr. L.: I do.

Uvani: This was his condition, and that is why it may
be for me perhaps necessary (terrific shaking of

medium at this point) to ask you to—deal—with this—personality yourself—while I withdraw—to create a little more quietude around the instrument. Our atmosphere, as you notice, is charged. . . . You will not be worried by anything that may happen, please. You will speak, if you can, with this one— and you will eventually return the instrument to my control.

Dr. L.: I will.

Uvani: Will you please to remember that you are dealing with a personality very young, tired, who has been very much hurt in life, and who was, for many years prior to his passing, unable—how you say—to think for himself. Now will you please take charge, so that I permit the complete control to take place. . . .

Uvani left the body of the medium at this point. For a moment, all life seemed gone from it as it lay still in the chair. Then, suddenly, another personality seemed to possess it. Slowly, the new personality sat up, hands violently vibrating in palsy, face distorted in extreme pain, eyes blinking, staring, unable to see anything at first, looking straight through us all without any sign of recognition. All this was accompanied by increasing inarticulate outcries, leading later into halting, deeply emotional weeping.

For about ten seconds, the new personality maintained its position in the chair, but as the movements of the hands accelerated, it suddenly leaned over and crashed to the floor, narrowly missing a wooden chest nearby. Stretched out on the floor before us, "he" kept uttering inarticulate sounds for perhaps one or two minutes, while vainly trying to raise himself from the floor.

One of Dr. L.'s crutches, which he uses when walking about, was on the floor next to his chair. The entity seized the crutch and tried to raise himself with its help, but without success. Throughout the next seconds, he tried again to use the crutch, only to fall back onto the floor. One of his legs, the left one, continued to execute rapid convulsive movements typical of palsy. It was quite visible that the leg had been badly damaged. Now and again he threw his left hand to his head, touching it as if to indicate that his head hurt also.

> *Dr. L.:* We are friends, and you may speak with us. Let us help you in any way we can. We are friends.
>
> *Entity:* Mhh—mhh—mhh—(inarticulate sounds of sobbing and pain).
>
> *Dr. L.:* Speak with us. Speak with us. Can we help you? (More crying from the entity.) You will be able to speak with us. Now you are quieter. You will be able to talk to us. (The entity crawls along the floor to Mr. Walker, seems to have eyes only for him, and remains at Walker's knee throughout the interrogation. The crying becomes softer.) Do you understand English?
>
> *Entity:* Friend . . . friend . . . friend. Mercy . . . mercy . . . mercy. . . . (The English has a marked Polish accent, the voice is rough, uncouth, bragging, emotional.)

I know . . . I know . . . I know. . . . (pointing at
Mr. Walker)

Dr. L.: When did you know him before?

Entity: Stones . . . stones. . . . Don't let them take me!

Dr. L.: No, we won't let them take you.

Entity: (More crying) Talk. . . .

Mr. Walker: You want to talk to me? Yes, I'll talk to you.

Entity: Can't talk. . . .

Mr. Walker: Can't talk? It is hard for you to talk?

Entity: (Nods) Yes.

Dr. L.: You want water? Food? Water?

Entity: (Shakes head) Talk! Talk! (To Mr. Walker)
Friend? You?

Mr. Walker: Yes, friend. We're all friends.

Entity: (Points to his head, then to his tongue.)
Stones . . . no?

Dr. L.: No stones. You will not be stoned.

Entity: No beatin'?

Dr. L.: No, you won't be stoned, you won't be beaten.

Entity: Don't go!

Mr. Walker: No, we are staying right here.

Entity: Can't talk. . . .

Mr. Walker: You can talk. We are all friends.

Dr. L.: It is difficult with this illness that you have, but
you can talk. Your friend there is Mr. Walker. And
what is your name?

Entity: He calls me. I have to get out. I cannot go any
further. I cannot go any
further. In God's name I cannot go any further.
(Touches Mr. Walker.)

Mr. Walker: I will protect you. (At the word "protect" the entity sits up, profoundly struck by it.) What do you fear?

Entity: Stones. . . .

Mr. Walker: Stones thrown at you?

Dr. L.: That will not happen again.

Entity: Friends! Wild men . . . you know. . . .

Mr. Walker: Indians?

Entity: No.

Dr. L.: White man?

Entity: Mh . . . teeth gone—(shows graphically how his teeth were kicked in)

Mr. Walker: Teeth gone.

Dr. L.: They knocked your teeth out?

Entity: See? I can't. . . . Protect me!

Mr. Walker: Yes, yes. We will protect you. No more beatings, no more stones.

Dr. L.: You live here? This is your house?

Entity: (Violent gesture, loud voice) No, oh no! I hide here.

Mr. Walker: In the woods?

Entity: Cannot leave here.

Dr. L.: Whom do you hide from?

Entity: Big, big, strong . . . big, big, strong. . . .

Dr. L.: Is he the one that beat you?

Entity: (Shouts) All . . . I know . . . I know . . . I know. . . .

Dr. L.: You know the names?

Entity: (Hands on Mr. Walker's shoulders) Know the plans. . . .

Dr. L.: They tried to find the plans, to make you tell,
but you did not tell? And your head hurts?

Entity: (Just nods to this) Ah . . . ah. . . .

Dr. L.: And you've been kicked, and beaten and stoned.
(The entity nods violently.)

Mr. Walker: Where are the plans?

Entity: I hid them . . . far, far. . . .

Mr. Walker: Where did you hide the plans? We are
friends, you can tell us.

Entity: Give me map.

(The entity is handed note pad and pen, which he uses
in the stiff manner of a quill. The drawing, showing
the unsteady and vacillating lines of a palsy
sufferer, is on hand.)

Entity: In your measure . . . Andreas hid. . . . (drawing)

Mr. Walker: Where the wagon house lies?

Entity: A house . . . not in the house . . . timber
house . . . log. . . .

Mr. Walker: Log house?

Entity: (Nods) Plans . . . log house . . . under . . .
under . . . stones . . . fifteen . . . log . . .
fifteen stones . . . door . . . plans—for whole
shifting of. . . .

Mr. Walker: Of ammunitions?

Entity: No . . . men and ammunitions . . . plans—I have
for French. . . . I have plans for French . . . plans I
have to deliver to log house . . . right where sun
strikes window. . . .

Dr. L.: Fifteen stones from the door?

Entity: Where sun strikes the window. . . . Fifteen
stones . . . under . . . in log house. . . . There I have
put away . . . plans. . . . (agitated) Not take again!

Mr. Walker: No, no, we will not let them take you
again. We will protect you from the English.

Entity: (Obviously touched) No one ever say—no one
ever say—I will protect you. . . .

Mr. Walker: Yes, we will protect you. You are protected
now for always.

Entity: Don't send me away, no?

Dr. L.: No, we won't send you away.

Entity: Protect . . . protect . . . protect. . . .

Dr. L.: You were not born in this country?

Entity: No.

Dr. L.: You are a foreigner?

Entity: (Hurt and angry, shouts) Yeah . . . dog! They
call me dog. Beasts!

Dr. L.: Are you German? (The entity makes a
disdainful negative gesture.) Polish?

Entity: Yes.

Dr. L.: You came here when you were young?

Entity: (His voice is loud and robust with the joy of
meeting a countryman.) Das . . . das . . . das! Yes . . .
brother? Friends? Pole? Polski, yeah?

Mr. Walker: Yes, yes.

Entity: (Throws arms around Walker) I hear . . . I
see . . . like . . . like brother . . . like brother . . .
Jilitze . . . Jilitze. . . .

Mr. Walker: What is your name?

Entity: Gospodin! Gospodin! (Polish for "master")

Mr. Walker: What's the name? (in Polish) *Zo dje lat?*

Entity: (Touching Mr. Walker's face and hands as he
    speaks) Hans? Brother . . . like Hans . . . like
    Hans . . . me Andre—you Hans.

Mr. Walker: I'm Hans?

Entity: My brother . . . he killed too . . . I die . . . I
    die . . . die . . . die. . . .

Mr. Walker: Where? At Tappan? Stony Point?

Entity: Big field, battle. Noise, noise. Big field. Hans
    like you.

Mr. Walker: How long ago was this battle?

Entity: Like yesterday . . . like yesterday . . . I lie here in
    dark night . . . bleed . . . call Hans . . . call Hans . . .
    Polski?

Mr. Walker: Did you die here?

Entity: Out there. . . . (pointing down) Say again . . .
    protect, friend. . . . (points at himself) Me, me . . .
    you . . . Andreas? You like Hans . . . friend,
    brother . . . you . . . Andreas?

Dr. L.: Do you know anything about dates?

Entity: Like yesterday. English all over. Cannot . . . they
    are terrible. . . . (hits his head)

Dr. L.: You were with the Americans?

Entity: No, no.

Dr. L.: Yankees?

Entity: No, no. Big word . . . Re . . . Re . . . Republic . . .
    Republic. . . . (drops back to the floor with an
    outcry of pain)

Dr. L.: You are still with friends. You are resting. You
are safe.

Entity: Protection . . . protection . . . the stars in the
flag . . . the stars in the flag . . . Republic . . . they
sing. . . .

Dr. L.: How long have you been hiding in this house?

Entity: I go to talk with brother later. . . . Big man say,
you go away, he talk now. . . . I go away a little, he
stays . . . he talk . . . he here part of the time. . . .

By "big man" the entity was referring to his guide, Uvani.
The entity rested quietly, becoming more and more lifeless
on the floor. Soon all life appeared to be gone from the
medium's body. Then Uvani returned, took control, sat up,
got back up into the chair without trouble, and addressed
us in his learned and quiet manner as before.

Uvani: (Greeting us with bended arms, bowing) You
will permit me. You do not very often find me in such
surroundings. I beg your pardon. Now let me tell to you
a little of what I have been able to ascertain. You have
here obviously a poor soul who is unhappily caught in
the memory of perhaps days or weeks or years of confusion. I permit him to take control in order to let him
play out the fantasy . . . in order to play out the fears,
the difficulties. . . . I am able thus to relax this one. It is
then that I will give you what I see of this story.

He was obviously kept a prisoner of . . . a hired
army. There had been different kinds of soldiers from

Europe brought to this country. He tells me that he had been in other parts of this country with French troops, but they were friendly. He was a friend for a time with one who was friendly not only with your own people, but with Revolutionary troops. He seems, therefore, a man who serves a man . . . a mercenary.

He became a jackboot for all types of men who have fought, a good servant. He is now here, now there.

He does not understand for whom he works. He refers to an Andre, with whom he is for some time in contact, and he likes this Andre very much because of the similar name . . . because he is Andre (w) ski. There is this similarity to Andre. It is therefore he has been used, as far as I can see, as a cover-up for this man. Here then is the confusion.

He is caught two or three times by different people because of his appearance—he is a "dead ringer" . . . a double. His friend Andre disappears, and he is lost and does what he can with this one and that one, and eventually he finds himself in the hands of the British troops. He is known to have letters and plans, and these he wants me to tell you were hidden by him due east of where you now find yourselves, in what he says was a temporary building of sorts in which were housed different caissons. In this there is also a rest house for guards. In this type kitchen he . . . he will not reveal the plans and is beaten mercilessly. His limbs are broken and he passes out, no longer in the right mind, but with a curious break on one side of the body, and his leg is damaged.

It would appear that he is from time to time like one in a coma—he wakes, dreams, and loses himself again, and I gather from the story that he is not always aware of people. Sometimes he says it is a long dream. Could it therefore be that these fantasies are irregular? Does he come and go? You get the kind of disturbance—"Am I dreaming? What is this? A feeling that there is a tempest inside of me. . . ." So I think he goes into these states, suspecting them himself. This is his own foolishness . . . lost between two states of being.

(To Mr. Walker who is tall and blue-eyed) He has a very strong feeling that you are like his brother, Sahib. This may account for his desire to be near you. He tells me, "I had a brother and left him very young, tall, blue-eyed," and he misses him in a battlefield in this country.

Now I propose with your prayers and help to try to find his brother for him. And I say to him, "I have asked for your protection, where you will not be outcast, degraded, nor debased, where you will come and go in freedom. Do as your friends here ask. In the name of that God and that faith in which you were brought up, seek salvation and mercy for your restlessness. Go in peace. Go to a kindlier dream. Go out where there is a greater life. Come with us—you are not with your kind. In mercy let us go hand in hand."

Now he looks at me and asks, "If I should return, would he like unto my brother welcome me? I do not think he will return, but if you sense him or his wildness of the past, I would say unto you, Sahib, address him as we have here. Say to him, "You who have found the God of your childhood need not return." Give him your love and please with a prayer send him away.

May there be no illness, nor discord, nor unhappiness in this house because he once felt it was his only resting place. Let there indeed be peace in your hearts and let there be understanding between here and there. It is such a little way, although it looks so far. Let us then in our daily life not wait for this grim experience, but let us help in every moment of our life.

Mr. Walker was softly repeating the closing prayer. Uvani relinquished control, saying, "Peace be unto you . . . until we meet again." The medium fell back in the chair, unconscious for a few moments. Then her own personality returned.

Mrs. Garrett rose from the chair, blinked her eyes, and seemed none the worse for the highly dramatic and exciting incidents which had taken place around her—none of which she was aware of. Every detail of what had happened had to be told to Mrs. Garrett later, as the trance state is complete and no memory whatsoever is retained.

It was 2:45 P.M. when Mrs. Garrett went into trance, and 4:00 P.M. when the operation came to an end. After some discussion of the events of the preceding hour and a quarter, mainly to iron out differing impressions received by the participants, we left Mr. Walker's house and drove back to New York.

On December 2, 1952, Mr. Walker informed me that

"the atmosphere about the place does seem much calmer."
It seems reasonable to assume that the restless ghost has at
last found that "sweeter dream" of which Uvani spoke.

In cases of this nature, where historical names and facts
are part of the proceedings, it is always highly desirable to
have them corroborated by research in the available refer-
ence works. In the case of "The Ghost of Ash Manor" (*Tomorrow*, Autumn 1952) this was comparatively easy, as we
were dealing with a personality of some rank and import-
ance in his own lifetime. In this case, however, we were
dealing with an obscure immigrant servant, whose name is
not likely to appear in any of the regimental records available for the year and place in question. In fact, extensive
perusal of such records shows no one who might be our
man. There were many enlisted men with the name
Andreas serving in the right year and in the right regiment
for our investigation, but none of them seems to fit.

And why should it? After all, our Andrewski was a very
young man of no particular eminence who served as ordinary jackboot to a succession of colonial soldiers, as
Uvani and he himself pointed out. The search for Andreas'
brother Hans was almost as negative. Pursuing a hunch
that the Slavic exclamation "*Jilitze . . . Jilitze . . .*" which the
ghost made during the interrogation, might have been
"Ulica . . . Ulica. . . ." I found that a Johannes Ulick (Hans
Ulick could be spelled that way) did indeed serve in 1779 in
the Second Tryon County Regiment.

The "fifteen stones to the east" to which the ghost
referred as the place where he hid the plans may very well

have been the walk leading from the house to the log house across the road. Some of these stone steps are still preserved. What happened to the plans, we shall never know. They were probably destroyed by time and weather, or were found and deposited later in obscure hands. No matter which—it is no longer of concern to anyone.

THE HAUNTED
NIGHTCLUB

Aptly named the Cafe Bizarre, this Greenwich Village artists' hangout was the scene of a seance held on the instigation of the owner, Rick Allmen, whose young wife, Renee, is apparently psychic.

On July 27, 1961, at two o'clock in the morning, she and her husband had been alone in the cafe, locking up. While already outside, she recalled having forgotten a package inside the place, and ran back alone. There was nobody in the dark cafe as she unlocked the doors again, yet she was overcome by an uncanny feeling of a "presence."

She put on the lights, took her package, and walked back toward the front door. Halfway down the long room, she glanced back toward the rear.

There stood an apparition, a man with piercing black eyes, wearing a white ruffled shirt of an earlier age, just staring at her. When she called out to him, he did not answer, he did not move. This was too much for the woman. Hurriedly she ran out of the cafe, locked up again, and told her husband what she had been through.

Together they returned once more, but there was no one in the place. A waiter working there had also met the stranger, it developed.

On the evening of the seance, about twenty people were present, including representatives of the *Journal-American*, the Associated Press, and two local papers. Mrs. Ethel Johnson Meyers was the medium, and I had carefully kept her in the dark about our purpose and destination.

Clairvoyantly at first, later in full trance, Mrs. Meyers described what she called a previous owner of the place, his son, and a girl that had been murdered.

Curiously enough, she described a man with penetrating dark eyes as the owner, and gave the period of 1804, and before. Yet she knew nothing of the apparition the owner's wife had seen. Also, she insisted that the house was different in those days, shorter; and that also was proven correct.

The initials of a man connected with the place were given as A. B.

In full trance the fact that the building was used as stables was brought out, also not known to the medium. Later, Richard Mardus, historian of the Village, confirmed that the place had been the location of the stables of Aaron Burr, who killed Alexander Hamilton in a duel.

THE
RIVERSIDE
GHOST

P lease help me find out what this is all about," pleaded the stranger on the telephone. "I'm being attacked by a ghost!" The caller turned out to be a young jeweler, Edward Karalanian of Paris, now living in an old apartment building on Riverside Drive.

For the past two years, he had lived there with his mother; occasionally he had heard footsteps where no one could have walked. Five or six times he would wake up in the middle of the night to find several strangers in his room. They seemed to him people in conversation, and disappeared as he challenged them on fully awakening.

In one case, he saw a man coming toward him, and threw a pillow at the invader. To his horror, the pillow did not go through the ghostly form, but slid off it and fell to the floor, as the spook vanished!

The man obviously wanted to attack him; there was murder in his eyes—and Mr. Karalanian was frightened by it all. Although his mother could see nothing, he was able to describe the intruder as a man wearing a white "uniform" like a cook, with a hat like a cook, and that his face was mean and cruel.

On March 9, I organized a seance at the apartment, at which a teacher at Adelphi College, Mr. Dersarkissian, and three young ladies were also present; Mrs. Ethel Meyers was the medium.

Although she knew nothing of the case, Mrs. Meyers immediately described a man and woman arguing in the apartment and said there were structural changes, which Mr. Karalanian confirmed.

"Someone is being strangled . . . the man goes away . . . now a woman falls and her head is crushed . . . they want to hide something from the family." Mrs. Meyers then stated that someone had gone out through the twelfth floor window, after being strangled, and that the year was about 1910.

In trance, the discarnate victim, Lizzy, took over her voice and cried pitifully for help. Albert, Mrs. Meyers' control, added that this was a maid who had been killed by a hired man on the wife's orders. Apparently, the girl had had an affair with the husband, named Henry. The murderer was a laborer working in a butcher's shop, by the name of Maggio. The family's name was Brady, or O'Brady; the wife was Anne.

After the seance, I investigated these data, and found

to my amazement that the 1812 *City Directory* listed an "A. Maggio, poultry," and both an Anne Brady and Anne O'Grady. The first name was listed as living only one block away from the house! Oh, yes—Mr. Karalanian found out that a young girl, accused of stealing, had killed herself by jumping from that very room!

THE
HAUNTED
CHAIR

B ernard Simon is a young writer with great interest in the occult, and very definitely a budding trance medium. He has done highly evidential trance work in a strange language that turned out, on later investigation, to be authentic medieval Inca speech of Peru, and he has had a number of astral projections as well as clairvoyant dreams.

His wife, Joan, who is known professionally on the stage under the name of Joan Lowe, and is the niece of screen luminary Joan Crawford, whom she greatly resembles, also had psychic talents in addition to her artistic ones. Over the past two years, we have shared a number of seance experiences.

A few weeks ago, the Simons moved into a brand-new building on West 12th Street. Shortly after their arrival,

Bernard found himself drawn to a certain neighborhood antique shop, where he saw a peculiarly shaped wooden chair. He immediately felt he must buy this chair, which was said to be of Mexican Indian workmanship.

He brought the chair, a thronelike seat with a round back, arm pieces and a strange base of crossed staves, to his newly furnished apartment, and thought no more of the peculiar force that made him acquire the unusual chair.

A few days later, Bernard awoke rather suddenly in the middle of the night from a deep sleep. There was enough light in the small apartment to distinguish solid objects from each other.

His eyes were drawn to the chair. In it sat an extremely tall man. His back was turned to the observer, but it was clear to Bernard that the man was unusually tall. Before he could get up and challenge the intruder, he had vanished into thin air.

Both Bernard and Joan Simon continually felt a "presence" and told me about their strange guest. I promised to arrange for a seance soon, and invited Ethel Johnson-Meyers to come down with me, without, however, telling her any of the details of the case.

On the morning of November 12th, I got an urgent telephone call from Joan. Something startling had just happened before her very eyes.

Her husband, laughingly and tongue in cheek, had remarked that he didn't believe in ghosts, and there was nothing to their "visitor." With that he got up and went to the kitchen, leaving Joan in the room.

There was a small but fairly heavy metal figurine, a pagoda, placed in the middle of a small table near one of the walls. As Joan looked on, that figurine *flew off* the table, and on to the floor, *with such violence that it broke in two*!

Three days later, the seance took place.

Mrs. Meyers took the chair, and within moments was in deep trance. Suddenly she sat bolt upright and Indian words came out of her mouth—words that Bernard immediately recognized as Quechua language, the dialect spoken in ancient Peru. Having learned a few words and prayer formulas himself, he managed to quiet the ghost.

It appeared that the man was Huaska, and that he recognized Bernard as his "son," apparently through reincarnation. He had been instrumental in getting Bernard to buy the chair, and then was anxious to make himself known. This having now been accomplished, there followed a joyful embrace, and then the Indian was gone.

The following day, all knocks and other strange noises that had accompanied the feeling of a "presence" prior to the seance were gone. The chair no longer moved and squeaked. All has been quiet since at the Simons'.

THE GHOST
AT THE
WINDOW

Out on Long Island, an expedition including Mrs. Meyers, Brian Flood (he edits the *New Voice*), Countess Catherine Buxhoeveden and myself descended upon a dilapidated manor house in the town of West Islip.

A man committed suicide there in 1948; many times since he has been seen at the window facing a busy highway; and several times, at night, motorists have seen him and, diverted momentarily from the road, crashed as a result.

On the second floor of the large wooden structure, Mrs. Meyers felt the presence of the ghost and stated that he had been shot in the left temple—this proved to be correct. At the same time, I had the distinct impression that the stock market had a great deal to do with his death.

Within minutes, we found a yellowed page from a newspaper, the investor's column, dated March 17, 1948; in the basement, the portrait of a well-known stockbroker was located.

A RENDEZVOUS
WITH HOUDINI

Every year on the anniversary of Houdini's death, a determined effort is made by the late escape artist's friend, Joseph Dunninger, to contact the departed, while at the same time giving a psychic the opportunity to obtain from the Other Side the code message contained in a sealed package in the possession of Mr. Dunninger, who is holding it in trust for a committee of scientists interested in obtaining positive evidence of Houdini's continued existence.

The group, which consisted of people from several countries, and laymen as well as scientists, met at the Park Sheraton Hotel in New York City at midnight on October 31, 1959. The Sensitive, who was to try to make contact with Houdini, was the well-known psychometrist Florence, of Edgewater, New Jersey.

Mr. Dunninger had brought along, in addition to a sealed code message, two pairs of handcuffs used by the late Harry Houdini in his work. Florence immediately seized upon one of these and said, "I am impelled to say, 'How much longer will I go on with this work?'"

Mr. Dunninger confirmed that this was indeed one of Houdini's favorite expressions. Florence, who knew Houdini slightly herself, then expressed a feeling of difficulty around the neck, and Mr. Dunninger confirmed that Houdini suffered in that region as a consequence of his work.

I then asked Florence, "Do you feel Houdini present among us?" and she answered in the affirmative. Touching the handcuffs again, she then said, "I get a man's name around him . . . Burke. . . ."

After a moment of reflection, in an effort to associate the name, Mr. Dunninger confirmed that Burke was one of Houdini's teachers of tricks.

Mr. Dunninger then asked Florence to describe some incident that might have puzzled the late Harry Houdini, who did not believe in Survival or Spiritualism.

Florence proceeded to describe "two balls breaking in half." Mr. Dunninger then confirmed that some years ago and unknown to the general public, Houdini had sat in a seance, at which time a departed medium friend of Houdini's was asked to give some evidence of her presence. The medium then materialized two spheres against a black background, which Houdini never was able to account for by so-called "natural" explanations. It was indeed a puzzlement to the great escape artist.

I then repeated a direct challenge to the spirit of Houdini to come forward and make contact, but nothing further happened.

Regretfully, Mr. Dunninger took the sealed envelope containing the code message, which incidentally carries a reward of 10,000 dollars, and hoped for better luck the next time.

ABOUT THE AUTHOR

Hans Holzer (1920–2009), "the Father of the Paranormal," wrote over 140 books on ghosts, witchcraft, and other paranormal subjects. He was most famous for investigating the site of the Amityville murders with the medium Ethel Johnson-Meyers in 1977, and was a consultant on Leonard Nimoy's acclaimed television show *In Search Of.*

GLEN COVE PUBLIC LIBRARY

3 1571 00325 7725

133.1097 Holzer, Hans, 1920-
H   2009.

     Ghost hunter.

DATE			

GLEN COVE PUBLIC LIBRARY
GLEN COVE, NEW YORK 11542
PHONE: 676-2130
DO NOT REMOVE CARD FROM POCKET

BAKER & TAYLOR